# WHEN THE GAME WAS JUST A GAME

## DAVID HOLLAND

PublishAmerica
Baltimore

ISBN: 1-60672-116-X
PUBLISHED BY PUBLISHAMERICA, LLLP
www.publishamerica.com
Baltimore

Printed in the United States of America

The three most important people in my life...
Cheryl, D.J., and Kelsey.

# ACKNOWLEDGMENT

My sincere thanks goes to all who have made this project possible. To all the coaches and athletic directors who have taken the time to give their insights, especially Mick Holland, Ron Rhen, Pat Flannery, Mike Rhoades, Mark Martino, Norm Brown, and Careen Caulfield.

To the many athletes who were willing to share their stories, especially Bill Murphy, Scott Hudson, Bob Killian, and Joe Muldowney.

To the young athletes with whom I've had the pleasure of spending time. I truly wish them the best of luck on their journeys through life.

To Ali Hobbs, Al Marshall, and Katie Halleron for their editing and candidness, without which this endeavor would never have been completed.

To my family: Cheryl, D.J., and Kelsey, who had to bear with me and teach me the "in's and out's" of computer technology and for their encouragement, love, and support.

# INTRODUCTION

Entering the new millennium, we seem to be constantly reminded of how life has changed from the simpler days of our youth. Lying in bed each morning, we envision the amount of e-mail we will have to answer when we arrive at our workplace and we make a mental note not to forget our cell phone that was left on the kitchen table the night before. It seems to take us a little longer to negotiate that first step toward the shower, and as we pass by the mirror we may tend to notice the hairline has retreated almost out of sight and the bulge around our middle has increased by the smallest of margins. The knees ache a little more these days, reminding us of the asphalt playgrounds and damp gymnasiums that we once called home, and a smile comes to our faces knowing that this wonderful soreness is a reminder of a time that we wouldn't trade for all the money in the world.

This book is for those of you who played in gyms that were not 94 feet long; gyms where you had to be careful when taking your jump shot that you didn't put too much arc less you might hit the ceiling or the track that often ran around the top. It's for those of you who remember wooden backboards and dead spots on the floor and when walls, not lines, were out of bounds.

This is for a special generation of players who wore Chuck Taylor Converse All Stars over two pair of Wigwam socks and your older brother's reversible high school practice jersey until it had holes in it. It's for those who remember great performances, and for those who recall local legends that tend to get larger and larger with each Friday night pitcher of beer when you're out with the old gang, and for those of you who claim to have shoveled every inch of snow off the playground court.

This book is for a generation gone by, a generation who looked at the game, and at life, with a much different perspective. For those of you who read it, I hope some bells will go off of a greater time, a time when a simple round ball did amazing things under the control of your fingertips and still gets the blood pumping every time you hear it bounce. For the kid in all of us who looked at this wonderful game for what it was, *A GAME.*

# FOREWORD

Basketball has always drawn the stereotype of being a city game. So many great players emerged from the concrete jungles to excel at the college, and later, the professional levels. Sports Illustrated and other, sports worthy, magazines ran stories about the playground legends that seemed to be bigger than life. New York City had the Rucker Tournament where stories were passed down of legendary games including the names of Herman the Helicopter, Pee Wee Kirkland, Tiny Archibald, and an up and coming star by the name of Connie Hawkins.

Growing up in Pennsylvania, we would read up on Philadelphia's Baker League where the pro's would mix it up with local stars at the same time Bobby Rydell, Frankie Avalon, and Fabian were cranking out hits which could be heard on WFIL A.M. radio or viewed every afternoon on American Bandstand. Philly produced some noteworthy players of its own: Wilt Chamberlain, Guy Rogers, Walt Hazard, and Paul Arizon, just to name a few.

I'm sure every city could boast of its hoops legends, for there was definitely a mystique attached to the high rise shaded playgrounds and the city streets that educated it's youth in terms of toughness and determination. But, in reality, the city did not have exclusive rights to the game. In a generation gone by, the game was bigger than the city. It was bigger than the streets and the legends. It was found in driveways, in church gymnasiums, and in parking lots. It was found in any playground with a hoop and a torn net and a neighborhood full of kids. It was found in lunch time pickup games and on Thursday nights in recreation centers where a bunch of guys would get together to rid themselves of the daily grind of the workplace. It was found in the beer leagues played by the older guys and the three on three games that would start at exactly 10 A. M. on Saturday mornings, where it was important to get there early because, *Winners Stay On.*

Some of these games still exist today, though it saddens me to say not quite as many.

And I'm willing to wager that if you do show up at a Thursday night pickup game anywhere in this country the odds are you'll find a few older guys still playing with the desire that only they can understand.

The game of basketball was once a way of life to thousands of kids from all walks of life. If baseball was America's pastime, basketball was America's soul. The requirements were minimal: a hoop attached to a barn door or telephone pole, a ragged pair of sneakers, a ball that would bounce as high as your waist and a simple dream.

What happened to this game that meant so much to a generation past? Why are the playgrounds empty? Why are high schools struggling to find enough players to foster teams? Why do 70% of the youth in our country quit sports by the time they're thirteen years old? What happened?

# THE PLAYGROUND

# THE PLAYGROUND

It was a very special place
I never will forget
It wasn't much to look at
Just a court, a hoop, a net

I wish I had a dollar
For all the memories it brought
The lessons that I learned there
The simple things it taught

Where grades were earned not given
In a way it was like school
But there were no formal teachers
And there were no formal rules

Where black and blues were cherished
And great moves all had their worth
Where a high five from an older guy
Was the greatest prize on earth

It was a place for players
No coaches showed you how
No parents ever came there
They were simply not allowed

The game was so important
To compete was all we knew
And win or lose we'd choose again
It's what we lived to do

What happened to these hallowed spots
Somehow they're not the same
I often just drive by them
With hopes to see a game

These places aren't important now
I'm sad to see it so
The game's become too organized
For reasons we all know

I'm saddened for the future
For the ones who'll never know
How great a place the playground was
Before the game became a show

—dah

Do you remember a time when the only organized game to be found was during the respective season long before there were exposure camps, weekend shootouts, AAU tournaments, and basketball schools? Do you remember the rivalries that would develop between local high schools before state regulations took them away by dividing schools into classes based on enrollment? Do you remember a time when you piled five guys into your father's car and drove to the next town, to play five guys that you knew would be at a certain playground at a certain time, and then agree to meet the following week at your own playground? Chances are that most of the players you competed against on those summer evenings or weekend afternoons were the same guys you would be playing against come December and January to standing room crowds in cramped little high school gyms.

Great friendships, that would last long after the ball stopped bouncing, were chiseled out of the respect earned on those hot summer nights.

There was a kind of pecking order that belonged solely to the playground, an unwritten rule that the older guys controlled the court at prime time, even if the younger guys were in the middle of a game. Prime time usually meant early evening, but it could materialize without warning, especially if that carload of players arrived unannounced and word spread that they were in town looking for a game. It was an understood fact that the young players would step aside, and it was accepted by everyone. It was okay if you were one of the young guys because you knew your time would come. I don't ever remember a kid running home to his parents to complain about the older guys kicking them off the court. In fact, it was great to be able to sit there and watch, and later imitate, some of the moves that the older guys brandished in those hotly contested pickup games. Young kids dreamed about a time when they would be the big shots, when a new generation of young kids would be sitting where they now sat, watching and admiring them. I'm not saying there wasn't some frustration. We often counted on the older guys showing up with a man short and hoping one of us might get picked into the game, but we understood how the process worked. The playground was theirs when they wanted it; after all, they too paid their dues. I remember my brother, Mickey, telling a story about the playground during his junior high school days. It seems he and his best friend went to the playground on a cold winter day, only to find the court covered with snow. They proceeded to shovel off the court, and as they completed the task a group of older players showed up and told them they were going to play. My brother, a little dejected, later walked into our house with a disgusted look on his face, and my father asked him if something was wrong. My brother, though not complaining, told my father the story hoping to get a little sympathy. My Dad, who was a basketball man himself, looked at my brother and simply said, "Get better and maybe they'll pick you".

I'm not so sure, in today's world, a father would handle a similar situation the same way. But that's the way the playground worked a generation ago, and I'm sure that the following day my brother and his friend were back at the playground, even shoveling if needed.

One young man who paid his dues to the playground and still revels in its magic is Mike Rhoades. Mike grew up in our hometown, living about twelve blocks from the playground. Though Mike was much younger than the players of our generation, it's safe to say that he viewed the game like an old-schooler. He often reminisces about his youth when he would dribble his ball to the courts every day, trying never to allow it to hit a crack in the pavement. Weekends, when the prime time games would start at one in the afternoon, Mike would make it a point to get to the playground by noon, hoping to be chosen. In his words, "it was demoralizing when the sides were picked, and I was not in the elite ten". But Mike, like everyone, waited his turn, realizing that it would come. I've heard him say, on more than one occasion, that as a kid the only goal he had, in regards to the game, was to get picked into the Prime Time games. Mike's goals progressed a little later in his life, in that he went on to an outstanding high school career, and later he led his Division III Lebanon Valley College team to the National Championship. Mike was named to the Division III All-American Team and was the Division III National Player of the Year. He is presently a very successful coach at

Randolf-Macon College in Ashland Virginia, where he was chosen ODAC coach of the year for two straight seasons. Mike speaks at a number of camps throughout the summer, and although I've heard him countless times, it never ceases to amaze me how excited he gets when he talks about the playground he grew up in and how it played such a significant part in his life.

To say that the playground taught us some valuable lessons would be an understatement. It was a kind of respect that everyone had. The playground rules were never contested by outside authorities. If there was a problem, it was settled then and there. If a call was made that didn't meet the approval of both sides, some choice words might be followed by a little trash talk but the game always would go on. Fathers were not found standing at the fence screaming at their kids or fighting with one another. Coaches were not manipulating the game, trying to keep their best players on the floor. There were no phonies or big timers. It didn't matter how you dressed, if you had new or old sneakers, or if your sox matched. You were judged and chosen simply by the way you played the game. The playground gave us a type of sanctuary, free from outside intervention, free to do nothing more than play, free to have fun doing something that we loved to do. It was as simple as that.

In those days, you did not need ten players. Half court games, two on two, three on three, four on four were just as competitive. The fact is you really didn't need anyone but yourself and your ball. I often tell young players that I was fortunate to grow up across the street from my playground. I tell them that I used to love being there by myself and allowing my imagination to go wild. Back in those days, UCLA was the dominant team year after year in college basketball. I would always imagine myself playing against UCLA with the game clock running down and my team losing by a point. I would make my move and take my jumper, and if I missed I always got fouled. I would stand on the foul line, imagining the T.V. cameras zooming in on me. The cheerleaders would be screaming, and the fans would be going crazy as I readied myself for my first free-throw. If I missed my first foul shot, then a player from UCLA would always jump in the lane too soon, and the referee would disregard the miss, and I would get to shoot again. If I made my first shot and missed my second, then we were going into overtime and the whole scenario would start again. When my team finally won, and we always did, I would run around the playground with my arms up in the air, totally oblivious to the world outside. I always get a laugh out of the kids when I tell a story of my mother and father, standing up at our front window observing me one day. When I hit the jumper to beat UCLA, and I proceeded to go through my victory celebration, my dad looked at my mom and said, "I think we may have a problem with him."

I ask you to take a ride some evening to one of the local playground around 6:00 p.m., prime time. I can almost guarantee that you will find some lonely places.

Kids today don't know what they're missing. I belong to a private swimming pool in our town. A few years back they built some basketball courts next to the swimming area. The courts have glass backboards and lines painted on them and they sit on top of a hill looking down over the pool. I often notice some of the local high school athletes hanging out at the pool, especially on weekends. One day, I approached one of the local stars and I asked him why he and his counterparts don't spend these weekend afternoons playing pickup games up on the courts. The boy responded that he comes up to the pool for some down time. He informed me that he had just returned from an exposure camp and his A.A.U. team was in a tournament the previous weekend. He also commented that his high school team was playing in a summer league and he had a game that night. He said that he came up to the pool for a couple of hours just to relax. He didn't even want to go in for a swim fearing that it might tire him out. My answer was, "I don't blame you". As I walked away I thought, "WOW!" This kid has a summer job—"Basketball". I actually felt a little sorry for the kid, as I sat back in my lounge chair and began to day dream about a summer when I was in junior high school, and we used to go down to our local pool. There was a basket that stood about nine feet tall, and on a Sunday we'd play all afternoon. It was great to play a game, take off your sneakers and socks, jump in the pool, then get out and do it all over again.

Families today live their lives according to a calendar that is attached to the front of their refrigerator. Players as young as junior high school and maybe even younger, wake up summer mornings and check the calendar to find out where their AAU tournament will be played the upcoming weekend. Parents schedule vacations around tournaments or cancel family vacations altogether because they cannot fit them into their child's schedule. This scenario is not restricted to just high school kids, but rather can dip as low as fourth-and fifth-graders.

Kids today very seldom just get together at the local playground to play pickup games. If they did, I'm sure they'd get a different perspective and a better feeling for the game. There were no All-Star teams chosen from those playground games. There were no parents coaching their kids and trying to pave the way for them. To the outside world, the playground seemed nothing more than a place to keep the kids off the street. To those who lived within its grasp, the playground was everything. It was more than just basketball; it was a classroom offering lessons in respect, humility, and character, and although it could be a rough place at times, it also had a way of teaching compassion.

There was a guy who hung out at the playground when I was young who taught me some important lessons that I carried throughout my life, ones for which I am eternally grateful. George was a down-syndrome kid who was quite a few years older than me. Every nice day you could set your watch to George's arrival at the playground. I can still see him walking down the street with his ball under his arm, wearing a pair of Chuck Taylor low cut Converse sneakers that always looked a few sizes too big. George loved Bob Cousy, and because of it he acquired the nickname Cous. Except for the prime time games, there was always a place for George in every pickup game. Even when the big games were being played, it never seemed to matter to George that he wasn't in there. He sat patiently with the rest of us and watched and learned. My house was across the street from the playground, and my Dad would often look out the window to check out the action. I often heard him comment, when seeing George playing the game that he loved, that basketball would probably prolong his life years beyond his life expectancy. I learned that our playground pal George passed away a few years ago. He was in his mid sixties. I guess my Dad was right, and I know that if there's a playground up in heaven, "Cous" is there every day, playing with the great ones and loving every minute of it. I'm sure that every playground can boast of stories similar to that of George, for the playground's identity was not just made up of great shooters and rebounders but of people. Some of the great stories get magnified as the years go by, but they never seem to lose their charm or mystique.

There was another guy who often showed up at our playground and everyone called him Doc. To say the least, Doc was a character. It was standard procedure for Doc to show up in his car and climb into the back seat which he proclaimed to be his locker room. We never knew what exactly would emerge from that locker room when the door opened. Once he had a net over his head, which he said would keep the bugs out of his eyes when he played. Another time Doc donned a pair of black shoes that he invented, believing they were "blister proof" and "sprained ankle proof." Doc's methods were a little out of sequence, but his love for the game was unchallenged. I remember one time sitting patiently at courtside, while Doc proceeded to give us a clinic on the five thousand plus ways to dribble a basketball. He started by putting the ball in his right hand and the clinic went as follows: dribble with your right hand low, right hand middle, right hand high, right hand low with a quarter twist, right hand middle with a quarter twist, right hand high with a quarter twist, left hand low, left hand middle, left hand high, and it went on and on if you get my drift. Doc's favorite move was called the One Step—Three Dribble Drive, and he would take great pride to teach it to anyone who would be willing to pay attention and learn it. God, how I miss those days!

Paying your dues often came with an age requirement. The older guys had the court at prime time, and if you were ever lucky enough to get chosen into one of their games you had to show that you could handle the pressure. Some of the young guys hated to play with certain playground veterans, since they blamed the youngsters for every errant pass. Every turnover that was committed invariably came their way. It didn't matter, in the least, if the young guy wasn't even around the play; he should have been there if the pass went out of bounds, or he should have picked a guy up on a switch that resulted in a basket. Some of the young guys took it personally and allowed it to bother them, but for most of us, it was just the natural order of how the playground worked. I always liked to think of it as "a rite of passage," an education in the truest sense of the game.

Very often, lessons in the playground were learned, not as much verbally as they were physically. I remember once in junior high school being picked to play in a half court game with some of the older guys. One of the players on the other team was just out of college, where he played for four years. I remember seeing this guy play when he was in high school, and I admit that he was kind of a hero of mine. I guess I was trying to impress him and some of the other older guys, and I started to get too cocky for my own good. I figured, with heading to high school the following year that it was time to show what I can do and prove to them that I belonged on the court with them. I truly believed that my time had arrived. It took all of about two possessions to realize how wrong I was. This hero of mine, who by the way outweighed me by about eighty pounds, set a screen on me with such force that it knocked me about ten feet in the air, only to touch down on the solid macadam court. He didn't even come over to ask if I was all right. Instead, he just stepped over me and checked it up as if nothing was out of the ordinary. The guy in question later became a teacher and a very successful high school coach. Many years later, I asked him if he recalled the hit he put on me, emphasizing that I never forgot it. He told me that he definitely remembered it, and that he did it on purpose. He said that he heard that I liked the game, and that I would eventually play for the high school team, and he wanted me to realize not only how important it was but how privileged I was to have such an opportunity. He told me that he wanted me to realize that no one is bigger than the game and that when players start to think that they're better than they are, there will always be a power screen or a stray elbow to remind them just where they stand.

Speaking of elbows, we also had a guy from our playground that had to have the sharpest elbows on the face of the earth. The joke was that he probably spent a half hour sharpening his bows before he came to the court. He also stood about six foot six, which brought his weapons about nose level to the average opponent, and there were very few players who ever escaped a lethal dosage of one or the other.

There was another physical presence who patrolled the unmarked lanes of our playground that I feel deserves mentioning. His name was Mike, but everyone called him Father due to the fact that he was our parish priest. Father Mike was a product of the Philadelphia School

System where he claimed to have played against Wilt Chamberlain. We had no reason to doubt him, after all he was a priest, and we figured his word was his honor. Father Mike was as physical a player as I ever remembered. Saying that he patrolled the lane may be an understatement. At six foot three and well over two hundred pounds, Father Mike was a force. There was no such thing as an easy basket when Father was on the opposing team, and, all too often, you paid the price if you tried to take it to the basket against him. It's hard to imagine, and I feel a sense of irreverence when I say his play sometimes ventured toward the borderline of being downright dirty. As I look back, it strikes me as funny the way everyone forgot he was a priest when the Roman Collar came off and the sneakers were laced up. Even the language, which was accepted in the playground, was never sugar coated for his sake, and I think I may have even heard a few choice words escape from his lips in the heat of battle. Father Mike was a competitor and a warrior on the court. I was often amazed on Sunday morning, sitting at eleven o'clock mass and listening to him recite his sermon, how he could be so devout and professional, knowing that in a few hours when the Sunday afternoon games would start, his demeanor would change and he would once again become just one of the guys.

I must admit, although I learned a lot from all the elders of the playground, there was one special older guy that taught me far more than anyone. Those of you, from a generation past, that had the good fortune to have had an older brother who was into the game know where I'm coming from. The lessons that were passed down from my big brother, by far, are the ones that I have most cherished throughout the years. Being four years my senior, he was everything I wanted to be. As a fifth grader, he was playing for the high school freshman team. By the time I played in eighth grade, he was in his senior year starting for the high school varsity. I simply idolized my brother growing up. I patterned my game after his. I shot my jumper exactly the way he did. I walked like he walked. I even tried to dress like him. I can still see him wearing his high school letterman jacket and often, when he wasn't looking, I would try it on and try to imagine what it would be like to someday have my own. My brother encouraged me and taught me but, like the other older guys, he made it a point that I would have to pay my dues and wait my turn. It seemed no matter how hard I tried, or no matter how well I did, he would always bait me with his famous line, "Yea, but you still can't beat me." Little did I know at the time that he was not only molding me as a player but also as a person. I remember some cherished advice he bestowed on me when I was in high school, a simple message that had become a cornerstone in my life. He said, "Remember that it's not enough to be a good player. There are plenty of good players, but to be a good player and a good person is to be a special kind of athlete." I've used that statement many times with players that I've coached over the years, and I often remind my own son and daughter to live their lives according to his advice.

The funniest story that ever happened between my brother and me occurred in our playground. Little did we know at the time it would be the last game that we would ever match up against each other. I was home from college on summer vacation, and he was out of school a few years and not playing as much as he once did. We matched up in a five on five game comprised of some pretty good local talent. I can still remember the crowd of people standing around the fence, watching the game, as well as a number of neighbors sitting out on their porches enjoying the hot summer evening. My father even took a few minutes from his office to come out on the porch and catch a little of the excitement, and he didn't have to wait too long for it to happen. About ten points into the game some trash talking started to develop between my brother and me. Nothing major, just statements like, *Hotshot college boy* and *Big Timer* retaliated by, *Has Been,* and after a made basket, *You can't check me, old man.* What followed I think surprised the both of us and completely changed the course of the game. My brother made a spin move and swung an elbow that caught me flush in the face. I remember grabbing the ball and throwing it at his head, and then all hell broke loose. We went at each other, swinging and swearing, forgetting our Catholic upbringing and forgetting that we were playing in a Catholic school yard, with the whole neighborhood watching and listening. After we were separated, the game continued to it's end, and we walked across the street, both sporting some cuts and swelling, but neither of us prepared to face what was waiting for us on our front porch. The realization of the seriousness of our behavior was written on our father's face. He proceeded to scream at the two of us like we were little kids, though both of us were in our twenties. Listening to him chastise us about ruining our reputations and embarrassing him in the neighborhood that he lived in his entire life was far worse than the bloody nose and the black eye. The next few days, it goes without saying, were pretty somber around our house. Nobody would dare mention the game, or anything else that took place that night.

About a week after the incident, I happened to be out with some friends, and as we entered this club I noticed my brother sitting at the bar. He motioned to me to come over and sit down. We hadn't spoken to each other since the incident, and the moment was a little awkward for both of us, until my brother said something I never thought I would hear coming out of his mouth: "I can't play you anymore". We both looked at each other and at the same time we burst out laughing. We spent the next hour talking about what a stir we created in the neighborhood, as well as in our house. I often wonder if our Dad was really as mad as he pretended to be or was he, deep down, a little proud of how we battled against each other that summer night so many years ago. I've told that story many times, and it always reminds me of the gratitude that I feel toward my brother for never giving me an inch. As I've said, he not only made me a better player, he made me a more driven man.

I'm sure every playground has its share of stories and unforgettable memories. It really was a special place. It was a unique haven where the realities of the world were never allowed to breed. Once you passed through its gates all that mattered was the game and the guys who were there to play it. The problems of the 60's; Vietnam, Civil Rights, the Cold War, were simply meant for another place. For the hours that we spent there, for the importance we placed on a simple game, for the camaraderie and laughter, for the competitiveness and humility learned there, I know I speak for thousands of others when I say that I'm truly grateful.

The game of basketball, in some ways, has just gotten away from us. The reason is not that the rules have changed or the kids have changed, the reason is that society has changed. There is way too much purpose to everything. For some unknown reason, whatever we deem important must have a final result. Kids play the game today for trophies, they play it for recognition, they play it for exposure. What they don't do is play the game for what it is, "A GAME".

# A Kid and His Court

A kid and his court
What more can be said
Floppy sox and old sneaks
A crew cut on his head

A worn out old ball
Tucked under his arm
As he enters his world
In this place free from harm

He takes a few dribbles
A soft jumper or two
There's such grace in his actions
His movements so true

There's a smile on his face
There's a gleam in his eye
In this world he's created
Free from hurt, scorn, and lies

He begins to get loose
As he works on his game
He's at peace with himself
There's no issues or blame

I could watch him all day
Going through his routine
Just this kid and his court
Just a boy and his dream

—dah

# THE HIERARCHY

# THE PROS

April 15, 1965—"Havlicek Stole the Ball! It's All Over!
Johnny Havlicek Stole the Ball!"

—Johnny Most

The 1965 Eastern Division Finals: 76ers v. Celtics, Chamberlain v. Russell, seventh game in the Boston Garden. The score is 110 to 109 the Celtics are up with five seconds remaining in regulation. Hal Greer, the great 76er guard set to inbound the ball, is looking for Chet Walker. Havlicek reads the play and knocks the pass away. Sam Jones recovers and dribbles out the clock. Celtics win by one point, and the Boston fans go wild, not to mention radio play by play man Johnny Most.

MAY 8, 1970—NEW YORK KNICKS—LOS ANGELES LAKERS—GAME 7 OF THE NBA FINALS!

Minutes before the opening tip, in front of a packed Madison Square Garden, Willis Reed, after missing game six with a torn muscle in his right thigh, hobbles onto the court in obvious pain. The crowd's going crazy as Reed takes a few warm-up shots. The game begins, and Reed scores the first two field goals, his only two baskets of the game, but his inspiration leads the Knicks to their first NBA Championship.

Prior to the game, Reed made the comment about facing a time when the game and the season was on the line, a time when one has to block out pain and contribute in any way possible. He commented on the fact that from the time he was young it's where he wanted to be, to be playing for a championship team. According to Reed, there was no way they were going to play that last game without him. He talked about the game and the pain and the realization that he had to play against a taller man who had just scored 45 points the previous game and he knew he had to play him on one leg. The moment Reed walked onto the floor that night, together with an outstanding professional career, solidified him as one of the greats of all time. It often amazes me how one individual can have an impact not only on a game and a city but on a sport itself. When the game ended and the reporters swarmed around Reed, he talked about knowing that he had to go out there that night and knew that all the applause, the feelings of the fans and the nice words that would later be written would mean nothing if his team lost. Talk about the heart of a champion; if you asked the basketball faithful of my generation to rank the greatest moment in NBA history, I'd be willing to bet Willis Reed's emergence from the locker room that night is at the top of most lists.

Wilt, Russell, West, the Big O, Elgin, Reed, the NBA as we knew it. When that era passed we were no less in awe of the Magic—Bird rivalry, the great Detroit Piston teams, and the emergence of the Chicago Bulls legacy led by Michael Jordan.

People often comment that the players today are better than they were a generation ago. Maybe! Certainly today's players are much bigger and stronger then ever before. They can jump higher and run faster, and they definitely have more tattoos and wear more jewelry than those of a generation past. But in terms of real players, I have to go back to a time when pro's spent most, if not all, of their careers with the same team. Growing up, I associated the Boston Celtics with Russell, Sanders, Sam and Casey Jones and Havlicek.

The 76ers roster consisted of stars like Greer, Luke Jackson, Chamberlain, Cunningham, and Chet Walker. The Lakers had West, Baylor, Goodrich. And the Knicks had Reed, DeBusschere, Frazier, and Bradley. To watch the Celtics run their fast break was poetry in motion. The Knicks making 7 or 8 passes before a shot went up was pure beauty. The game was teamwork and the marquee was the player's ability to put the team above individual achievement.

One of my favorite pastimes is to question basketball fanatics as to the greatest team that could ever be assembled. I love to hear different generations give their renditions. My father's team was Bob Petit, Bob Cousy, Dolph Schayes, Joe Fulks, and the big young kid from Philadelphia, Wilt Chamberlain. Very seldom will you ever get an agreement, and the arguments over this question usually attest to one's age group. Another interesting topic for discussion when in the midst of basketball experts is, "who was the greatest player of all time?" It's hard not to pick Jordan with all his accomplishments. Bird, Magic, and Jabbar certainly receive a righteous amount of votes. I personally, and it may give my age away, choose Oscar Robertson. The "Big O" simply did everything. He could shoot, handle the ball, pass, and play defense. He was the king of the triple double (double figures in points, assists, and rebounds). He made everyone around him better and he did it with his game, not with his mouth or his with his fancy play.

The youth of the NBA is slowly dragging the production of the pro game downward. According to a U.S.A. report in December of 2002, in the last twelve NBA drafts, only five first-round picks completed four years of college. In the 2001 draft, four of the first ten players selected—No. 1 Kwame Brown, No. 2 Tyson Chandler, No. 4 Eddy Curry, and No. 8 DeSagana Drop—were high school students. This does not even address the number of college kids who leave early and are not chosen in the first round.

In order to assess some of the damages associated with the game today, we have to take a serious look at the game from the top down. The professional game is getting younger and younger. So many players are leaving college or jumping right from high school, and the affects are seeping down to the lowest, or should I say youngest, levels of the game. The level of performance in the pros has suffered, not to mention the number of players who give up their amateur status and never see the lights of the professional arena. The dreams of young players have fallen under the control of older, though I'm not sure wiser, influences who project them into stardom long before they are physically and mentally ready. Team unity in the professional ranks seems to be a forgotten entity. Free agency has moved players around so much that the average fan has lost that "die hard" monogram that once constituted a favorite team. Showmanship and style rank much higher than fundamentals, and impacts greatly the countless number of youth who tune in to view the players at the highest level of the game.

Aside from the "overwhelming presence of adolescent athletes", there are other problems affecting the pro game today. Roster changes take away so much team chemistry that the pro's, for the most part, have turned into a one on one challenge. The team concept seems to be a forgotten entity. Some coaches profess the passing game; Byron Scott had the New Jersey Nets a few years ago setting back screens and moving without the ball and was very successful, but he is in the minority. Maybe people don't want to see that kind of basketball anymore. I still loved to watch Reggie Miller move without the ball. I enjoy watching Eric Snow, Steve Nash, and Jason Kidd run the point and dish it off, but I just don't think there's enough of that kind of play throughout the league. I realize that change is inevitable, but I thoroughly enjoy hearing an announcer refer to a player as being, "old school." I believe it's a compliment to be recognized as someone who does all the little things without the flash and show. John Stockton recently retired and I, for one, am sad to see it. Stockton epitomized "old school" basketball in a "new school" world. I marveled at the way he saw the floor, how he always seemed to be thinking ahead. More than anything I loved watching his demeanor. Very seldom did you see Stockton lose his cool. He never went off on a teammate for missing one of his passes, and he never outwardly got down on himself after committing a turnover.

In his last season I took my son to Philadelphia to see Stockton and the Jazz play the 76'ers. I wanted my son to see him play, and I felt that I owed it to myself to see the end of an era. I told my son to watch the little things that he does. Watch him warm-up, I told him. Watch how he even takes his lay-ups seriously. Watch how he runs to the bench when there's a time out. Even though the Jazz lost the game, it was still a great night out for father and son. Stockton's demeanor and his work ethic are what most fathers would love their sons to see, night in and night out, when they tune into an NBA game. As I left the Wachovia Center, I couldn't help but feel proud to have seen Stockton play before he made his journey to Springfield and took his place among the many great *Old Schoolers*.

The length of the professional season takes its toll on

the production and effort put forth by the players' night in and night out. I've often heard the comment, "I don't like watching the NBA because they don't play hard until the fourth quarter." The statement doesn't apply to all players, but there are some who find a comfortable pace at which to perform. A high school coach once made the statement that he likes to watch the NBA playoffs, as opposed to the regular season, due to the fact that the scores are much lower than during the regular season, because the pro's actually get down and play some defense.

Arguments over the length of the season are not going to change it. Inflated salaries, generating revenue, and new arenas are all part of the modern game and the society that has embraced it. I, personally, still like to watch the pro game, but I don't love it the way I did in my youth. The NBA is big business and the game itself has taken a hit because of it. I once talked to an NBA player of a generation past who, do to his limited ability, only lasted a few years. I asked him what it was like to play with some of the high priced stars of his day. He said, that back then most of the guys played because the really loved the game. There were a few who abused the privilege by missing practices or showing up late, but that was rare. Sure, we traveled a lot, but we traveled first class, stayed in first class hotels, and ate first class food. When you come right down to it, the job itself wasn't that tough for the money they were paying us to play it.

# COLLEGE

Bruins—Houston (Alcindor—Hayes)
Pistol Pete, Calvin Murphy, Rick Mount
John Wooden—Can Anyone Beat UCLA?

College basketball, like the pro's, is going through a transition period that is not only reshaping the college game but also reshaping the importance of amateurism. I grew up in a small coal mining town in Pennsylvania about two hours northwest of Philadelphia. Although the Sixers were the professional team from the big city, they played second fiddle to most of us within the viewing area because they were in the same town as the "BIG FIVE". The BIG FIVE consisted of the University of Pennsylvania, Saint Joseph's, LaSalle, Temple, and Villanova, and every Wednesday and Saturday night there was a double header aired on our local Channel 17 from the greatest gymnasium in the country: THE PENN PALESTRA. There were legacies of the BIG FIVE. There were shoes to fill, and comparisons to make, as to the greatest players to ever wear the uniform of the respected schools. Players like

Paul Arizon of Villanova, Tom Gola of LaSalle, and Guy Rogers of Temple, set the benchmark for players of my generation who represented these schools in the Quaker City.

When I was a young kid, the announcer for the BIG FIVE games was Les Keiter. Les was the greatest play by play man I have ever heard. He coined phrases like", Tickles The Twine" which he emphatically proclaimed every time a player swished a jumper. Whenever he would announce the score it would always be, "The Arithmetic Reads", and "In again, Out again, Finegan," denoted a shot that almost went in.

My favorite memory of Les Keiter goes back to a game played between Villanova and St. Bonaventure's. I can still recall sitting in my living room watching the game with my dad, when the center of St. Bonaventure, a big left hander by the name of Bob Lanier, who later went on to a very productive professional career, stole the ball and proceeded down the court on a break away lay-up. It happened so fast that I even think it surprised Keiter who screamed into his microphone and into our living room, "There He Goes, The Big Cat, Going Coast to Coast on a One Man Sashay!"

There was simply nothing like the Big Five. The thought of playing for a Big Five team some day, and it didn't matter which one, was the dream of every kid who owned a basketball and grew up in Northeastern Pennsylvania. My senior year in high school I was coached by Stan

Wlodarczyk, who played on the 1969 LaSalle team that only lost one game. I still remember making the two hour trip down the PA. Turnpike and the Philadelphia Expressway to 33rd Street to see them play.

The Palestra was what college basketball was all about. Following the first basket scored by each team, the floor would be bombarded with paper streamers brandishing each team's colors. It was tradition. To the officials working the game it was no big deal. No technical fouls were called; just sweep off the court, and let's get on with the game. If there was anything louder than the Palestra on a night when two Big Five teams matched up, then I'd have to hear it. They can say what they want about Duke and Carolina, but if you wanted rivalries you had to be on the Penn Campus, in the Palestra, when two Big Five teams squared off in the 1960's.

A Philadelphia Daily News article—The Collegians— written by Dick Jerardi—02/06/2002 sums it up best:

> "College basketball in this city is a feeling. You can't see it on television. You can't hear it on the radio. You can't be told about it. You need to be there."

> There are the two national championships (La Salle, 1954, and Villanova, 1985), the nine Final Fours (Villanova three times, La Salle and Temple twice each, Penn and St. Joe's once each), the four Hall of Fame coaches (Penn's Chuck Daly, St. Joe's Jack Ramsay, and

Temple's John Chaney and Harry Litwak), the two Hall of Fame players (La Salle's Tom Gola, Villanova's Paul Arizon), the five national players of the year ( Arizon, St. Joe's George Senesky, and La Salle's Gola, Michael Brooks and Lionel Simmons). It can't be explained by reading about it. It can't be understood by asking questions. Old films don't really illuminate it. It helps a little to walk around the Palestra a few dozen times, savoring the walls that are adorned with the building's history."

There's no hiding the fact that larger conferences have taken over today's college agenda. Big business has turned the college game into a multi-million dollar showcase.

Television and national prominence have taken away from regional rivalries. The NCAA Tournament and the Final Four have become as big, if not bigger, than the World Series and the Super Bowl. I still remember, prior to the 65 team national tournament, when there was another post season playoff that has lost some of it's notoriety in recent years, the National Invitational Tournament (NIT) held each year in New York's Madison Square Garden. They still have the NIT, now made up of teams that come close but don't get chosen for the Big Dance. I still enjoy watching the tournament, though it has lost a little of its luster in the eye's of most of today's fans who only want to see the best.

I can still remember when the NIT was a big time tournament. My dad would take us to New York for the weekend of the semi-finals and finals, and I can still recall games played in the Old Garden, then later in the new one. I can still see the likes of Vinny Ernst, JoJo White, Pistol Pete Maravich and Dean Meminger. I remember the tournament in the mid 1960's, when two guards by the names of Bobby Lloyd and Jim Valvano led their Rutgers team, a sentimental favorite, into the final weekend only to come up short. The team that took home the trophy that year was Southern Illinois, led by the tournament MVP Walt Frazier, who would later play a few more games in the Garden.

The dream of playing at the college level was once enough to inspire high school kids to work on their skills and their fundamentals—the little things that could make them better players. The high school coach and the players' parents were there to help along the way. To be given the opportunity to play for a college for four years was the dream of most high school players. Kids, a generation past, didn't leave college early, and they played on the varsity for just three seasons. Every college and university had a freshmen team, and every freshman, regardless of talent, played on it. Freshmen teams were important. They were not just indoctrination into the college game but indoctrination into the whole college scene, including academics. Today, the major programs seldom have a great player who stays around for four years. There have been exceptions in the likes of Duke's Shane Battier and Wake Forest's Tim Duncan, but they head a short list. More and more college players today look at the college experience as nothing more than a stepping stone. Each year, players with less and less talent are leaving at an alarming rate, some after their freshmen season, a season that wouldn't have put them in a varsity uniform a generation ago. A few years back, there was some discussion about bringing back the freshman mandatory requirement with the hope that more student athletes might remain on campus for at least another year, in order to mature both physically and mentally. The rule never did materialize, and by the way college basketball is progressing, in terms of a business perspective, I'm willing to bet it never will.

Some view the NCAA as a type of monopoly, controlling the flow of income generated by the players who do not share in the rewards. Many believe college players' should be paid for the amount of time and money they bring into their respective schools.

College coaches are under the microscope now more than ever. In October 2003, The National Association of Basketball Coaches ordered all 327 Division I head basketball coaches to attend a meeting in Chicago, to discuss how to repair damages brought on by scandals involving coaches and their programs. Several coaches over the past years have been dismissed, with some facing criminal charges. From allegations of coaches' fraternization with female students and drinking at student parties, to academic fraud, to reports about a murdered player, the college game has recently been upgraded from the sports page to the front page. Although it's unfair to chastise the entire college coaching profession for the fraudulent behavior of a few, the skepticism and the publicity that is generated bring the entire coaching community under the microscope.

The money generated by television coverage of the men's national tournament is estimated to be in the billions over the next ten years, with much of the proceeds going to the teams participating. Coaching salaries are often determined by their team being chosen for the 65 team field. The pressure placed on winning becomes very cut and dry. If a coach doesn't consistently win and get his team to the Big Show, regardless of the fact that he may run a clean program, he may still be faced with an early retirement. A mediocre season does not add to his longevity, nor do the expectations that accompany the big salaries and national exposure show little tolerance for failure?

Aside from all the negative publicity, the average college basketball fan still can't help but get caught up in the excitement of the college game. What pulls us in is the Cinderella Team that fights its way to the sweet sixteen round of the tournament, as do the human interest stories that broadcasters reveal, dealing with the hardships that many of the college athletes had to overcome in their quest for stardom.

Regardless of the early departure rules and the rise in negative publicity, most fans still view Division 1 college basketball as the ultimate in amateur sports. The excitement of the college campus on Game Day is unchallenged. To watch a Duke game and listen to the Cameron Crazies is enough to make anyone, outside of Carolina Blue, a fan. To listen to Dick Vitale announce, time and time again, that he has the greatest job in the world, has many of us wondering if he just may be right. I miss the partnership of Vitale and Jim Valvano, as well as the team of Billy Packer and Al Maguire of the 1970's and 1980's.

Color commentary has always added to the excitement of the game, and the loss of Valvano and Maguire has been felt by all true college basketball fans. I actually had the opportunity to meet Coach Valvano many years ago and, to say the least, it was a memorable experience. I was working at the summer basketball camp of my former Holy Cross coach, George Blaney, at the time. One afternoon, Coach Blaney pulled me aside and asked me if I'd mind driving into Boston to pick up Coach Valvano, who was flying in to speak at camp that afternoon. At the time, Valvano was the coach of Iona, prior to his N.C. State days. I'll never forget our ride back to Worcester that afternoon. Coach V was on a roll. I thought he was the funniest guy I've ever been around, and I couldn't wait to hear his talk. When we arrived at The Cross and Valvano took the floor I was mesmerized, as were a couple hundred campers, by his message and his sincerity. He talked about the difference between the Big Timers in the game and the Real Players. He talked about the type of player he wanted in his program, and by the time he was finished every kid in the gym was aching to get into a game and take a charge. Over the past twenty five years, I've worked more camps and heard more speakers than I care to remember, and I can say with admiration that I have never heard a greater camp speaker than I heard that afternoon.

I also remember hearing Coach Valvano, speaking on television, many years later trying to raise funds for the Jimmy V Foundation, set up to battle the very disease that was slowly taking his life. It's strange how a simple message can have such a lasting impact. I'll never forget his final words that night as I sat in my reclining chair with tears running down my face listening to Jimmy V say, "I know I got to go, but I have one last thing. I've said it before and I'm going to say it again—Cancer can take away all my physical abilities. It cannot touch my mind; it cannot touch my heart; and it cannot touch my soul and these three things will carry on forever."

The college game has always been made up of people like Valvano. People like Pete Corrill at Princeton, with his famous passing game. People like John Wooden, who taught his players much more than the importance of winning, His Pyramid of Success became the cornerstone of coaches throughout the country. The college game today needs to reflect on some of the positives that made it great. How we all looked forward to the varsity seasons of players like Lew Alcindor ( Kareem Abdul Jabbar), wearing the blue and gold of U.C.L.A. and knowing that he would be around for his entire college career; how we watched Al Maguire pace the sidelines of Marguette, how we saw the genius of Dean Smith's four corner offense; how we watched U.C.L.A. play with such precision, and to know that big time programs recruited players to fill their needs knowing that the players would be around for the distance.

Has any other intercollegiate sport been depleted of its athletes to the extent of college basketball? College football players are forced to remain in school for a specific number of years under an NFL policy. Although that rule will probably be challenged by an exceptional running back or a prolific passer that could be a first round draft pick, the fact remains that it still exists and has given college football a sense of stability.

Big time college basketball is in trouble and will continue to decline with the number of departures. The game will never get back to where it once was, and I, for one, am sad to see it so. Big time college basketball has lost something special, the simplicity of the game in all its beauty.

There is a redeeming factor in the fact that Division I basketball is not the only college game in town. In the year

2000, John Feinstein wrote a book, "The Last Amateurs—Playing for Glory and Honor in Division 1 Basketball." Feinstein followed the programs of the Patriot League which, at the time, consisted of Army, Navy, Colgate, Holy Cross Bucknell, Lehigh, and Lafayette. Being a graduate and former player from Holy Cross, and sharing a long friendship with Pat Flannery, the coach of Bucknell, drew me to the book, and I couldn't put it down. Feinstein does an outstanding job of depicting life both on and off the court of these outstanding schools, and he gives the reader a sense of hope that there still may be some integrity left in the college game. In the introduction to his book, Feinstein admits, before deciding on the Patriot League, he wrestled with the idea of writing about the Ivy League and even Division III Basketball.

I happen to be a great fan of Division III, having a niece who played for a fine program and a nephew who's making a name for himself as the coach of Randolf-Macon College's men's team. I encourage basketball fans to check out the caliber of basketball played at the Division III level. I mentioned Pat Flannery earlier. Pat and I have been friends going on thirty years. Prior to his tenure at Bucknell, Pat was the Head Basketball Coach at Lebanon Valley College, where his team captured the national championship in 1994. I'll never forget the excitement of that season, and their run through the playoffs.

Home games at Lynch Gymnasium on the LVC campus in Annville, PA. were packed to the rafters. Rivalries with schools like Franklin and Marshall and Elizabethtown were anticipated and talked about for weeks prior to the games. I remember making the trip to Buffalo, N.Y., in a snowstorm, to be at the Final Four, where I was joined by a large contingent of Lebanon Valley fans, all believing that their Dutchmen had a real shot at capturing the crown. I'll never forget that Saturday night, when the final buzzer sounded and the National Championship was theirs, how players', families, and friends stormed the court in celebration. Observing the faces of the Division III National Champs, I came to the conclusion that the thrill of victory greatly overshadowed the Roman numeral that distinguishes college classes. These young men didn't care what division they represented, they were cutting down the nets as the best team in the country.

Mike Rhoades, who played on the team, remembers the night and his entire Division III career like it was yesterday. Mike speaks of his days at LVC as the greatest time in his life. I once asked him what he would give to be able to go back to that time period, and Mike answered jokingly, "Body Parts". He talks about the friendships, the closeness of the community, the school itself, and the basketball that far surpassed anything imagined upon his graduation from high school. "There's not a week goes by that I'm not on the phone with one or more of my teammates. My wife, a former LVC field hockey player, and I still attend many of the alumni functions, knowing we'll be reacquainted with so many old friends."

Many people may look at the basketball played at the Division III level and label it substandard in regards to the bigger classes, but to the players who play and the coaches who coach it's the most important game in town. Programs can be constructed on needing players at particular positions, rather than on pure athletic ability. Players are going to stay around for four years, which in turn allows systems to take hold and create not only basketball teams but also basketball memories.

My close relationship with a number of Division III coaches has only strengthened my belief that the D-III game is in great hands. Coaches recruit with a passion and, although their budgets are far less than their higher level counterparts, their determination and willingness to spend long hours on the road as well as in the office is, to say the least, noteworthy. There also seems to be a closer relationship between player and coach at the D-III level. Coaches and players often work together on fund raising campaigns and school sponsored projects that not only affect their sport but the entire athletic program of their respective schools. Players perform community service hours and often work as ushers and attendants at other sporting events. Coaches, who are rarely under sneaker contracts, are constantly wheeling and dealing to get the best product for the best price.

I recently read an article about a local Division III coach who believed, as most do, that D-III was a stepping stone to moving up the coaching ladder. The story goes on to say that ten years later the coach is still with the same program and couldn't be happier. The article actually starts out with a story of the coach calling a local restaurant trying to arrange a meal for his players, hoping to persuade the manager to change the Wednesday night chicken wing special to Monday night. You have to love his commitment to his players, and if you're a real basketball person you can see why the coach doesn't want to move on. The closeness, the camaraderie, the game behind the game, makes it all worth while.

While the talent level in Division I is dwindling due to the rising early departure rate, the talent level of Division III is escalating. Some high school players, who really want to play at the college level, are giving in to their egos and opting to play for the lower division. It's also not uncommon for D III teams today to have more than one player on their team who started out in a higher division and, seeing the writing on the wall, decided to move down, and, for most of the journeymen, the decision has proven to be the right one.

I have a niece who competed for four years at a fine Division III school in Pennsylvania. She was the starting point guard on her team, and she enjoyed every aspect of her college life. Jamie and I have a great relationship, and we often worked out together in the off season. Our workouts would always end with a heart to heart talk that covered just about any topic. During her last season we also kept in touch via the Internet, where we discussed her team and its progress. Prior to the New Year 2004, her team was struggling a bit, and I could tell she was a little down in the dumps, so I e-mailed he the following message:

Jamie,

Been following the season on d3hoops, and I see that things aren't going quite the way you expected. Sometimes life throws us those curve balls that we have trouble dealing with, and we just can't understand why things aren't exactly right. But I'll tell you what kid, *THAT'S LIFE.* If everything always came easy we would never be able to appreciate the accomplishments when they do come along. I know that right now you're searching for answers, but the only real answer is to keep looking forward, because the past is exactly that. There's going to be more trying times ahead but also a lot more happy times. What we all need to do is not allow those tough times to dominate us, to always remember that the sun will rise tomorrow, and a new day will bring new challenges. Be thankful for the good things and work hard to over come the bad— that's *CHARACTER.*

I told Jamie that a few years ago I spoke at a banquet for a high school team that had a very successful season. I ended my talk to a team, made up of some pretty special girls, with these words:

Believe in your abilities, because you have ability.
Believe that you can make a difference in the world, because you can make a difference.
Believe in achieving more than you can achieve, because there are no such things as limitations.
Believe in friends, because you need them.
Believe in your heart, because it will never lie to you.
Believe in your family, because they are the source of all your power.
Believe in laughter, because it heals wounds.
Believe in dreams, because they can come true.
Believe in miracles, because they happen every day.
Believe in God, because He's real.
Believe in yourself, because you're worth believing in.

I signed off by wishing her the best with the remainder of the season and with the remainder of her school year. A week or two later I received an e-mail from Jamie that said,

Hey Uncle Dave,

We started the New Year off with another win... We're playing the way we should, and it's fun. I'm pretty excited about the remainder

of the season. Just wanted to say thanks and
I'll be in touch soon.

It's Fun! The most important words and the two words most D-III players focus on. D-III players are not about scholarships or professional contracts. They play because of the game, period. They put in the same amount of time as their D-I counterparts. They spend countless hours at practice and in the weight room. They run in the off season and they do it because they want to not because they're bound by scholarship. Sometimes they play in front of capacity crowds and sometimes they play to a crowd of thirty. Some D-III programs don't even charge admission to their games. But the players still play hard. D-III athletes are students first, their future depends on it. Most D-III coaches' check on grades not because they may lose a projected started for an upcoming game but because they want to see their players succeed in a life after college. These players play for their teammates, their fans, and their friends but more important they play because of a burning desire to compete. Its true passion and it can be seen on their faces when they leave the gym on a cold night and drag themselves back to their dorm rooms exhausted only to spend time with their books. It can be seen after a tough defeat with tears running down their faces. And it can be seen with the jubilation of victory that only the true athlete understands. Division III is athletics, there's no other way to describe it. My hat goes off to all the D-III athletes for being what they are and doing what they do.

# High School

Do you remember getting your first pair of team sneakers? Those Chuck Taylor high top Converse were the most treasured piece of equipment that a high school player possessed. Every team wore them, and they were proudly adorned with shoelaces of your school colors.

Do you remember when gym bags were not the size of suitcases and were not thrown over your shoulder, but rather had a zipper and two handles and sported your school name and emblem on both sides? Packing that little bag every morning before departing for school was a work of art. I can still remember my daily ritual as I checked its contents by repeating the words, "Sneakers, Socks, Jock, Pants, Shirt, and Towel".

Do you remember playing in gymnasiums the size of classrooms packed to the rafters with screaming fans? Do you remember a time when high school basketball was the most important game in town? Do you remember that to be a member of a high school team, where you would have the chance to run through a paper hoop onto the court as the band played and the cheering section exploded, was like no other feeling on earth?

High school hoops was not just a school function, it encompassed the whole community. To do battle with the rivals from the neighboring town was the topic of discussion in every barber shop, bar room, and coffee house. Standing in line to get into such a game could last for hours. Since the capacity of most high school gyms was considerably low, this only added to the noise and excitement for those fortunate enough to get inside.

High school players were looked at with a sense of admiration. They were the heroes to the youth of their respective towns, who dreamed of one day walking in their shoes. Fathers often set them up as role models for their kids. High school girls smiled and blushed as they passed by them in the halls of school. They were the kings of the soda shops when they entered wearing their letterman jackets.

Somehow, I'm sad to say, the high school game has lost a little of this innocence and, with it, a little of its magic. High school dreams of playing for your high school varsity, and maybe even getting a chance to play at the next level, have been surpassed by thoughts of skipping college and heading right to the pros.

The high school team is not the only game in town anymore, and maybe not even the most important in the eyes of the high school athlete. Many high school teams who compete in local summer leagues do so without certain team members who are committed to summer traveling squads made up of elite players from many different regions. AAU coaches today have as much say, if not more, about a player's development and future plans, than the high school coaches. College coaches, who once had to impress a recruit and his or her parents, are now facing not only family but a number of coaches who have had a part in the player's basketball development. Summer exposure camps and weekend shootouts are becoming more important to the high school player than the neighboring town rivalry, played in a high school gym on a Tuesday or Friday night in January.

I am not totally against AAU or traveling basketball teams. I would be a hypocrite to say so, as I actually coached an *Athletes for Better Education* team made up of eighth grade boys. I honestly think the AAU experience can be very beneficial. There's no questioning the fact that it allows kids to play with teammates who are really into the game. It also provides players with an opportunity to meet other kids and to compete at a very high level. The team that I coached played in a total of just three tournaments. We practiced once a week, we scrimmaged some local teams. Although we had the opportunity to compete in more tournaments, I'm convinced that it was plenty for kids at their grade level. Total commitment, which consists of tournaments almost every weekend, should be reserved for only high school age players, and only if it truly is what they want to do. Summer vacations dominated by weekend tournaments, for players of elementary and middle school age, can leave a big void in the social development of most kids. I believe the average elementary and junior high school athlete will eventually get tired of the rigorous schedule, thus affecting his or her play, not to mention his or her enthusiasm for the game itself. Saturation of anything can eventually have a negative affect and, in the case of the young athlete, cause many to simply get tired of playing, escalating the dropout rate.

There also needs to be communication between traveling squads and high school programs, and maybe even some standardized guidelines that coaches must follow.

I recently sat down with the parents of a high school player whose team was still alive in the high school playoffs in March. There son, a starter on the squad, was having a pretty good season but was concerned about whether he would be able to hook up with an AAU team for the spring and summer. The year before he played for a regional team, but it looked as though there would not be enough players, due to age limitations to comprise this team again. Searching the Internet he found two teams within driving distance that were holding tryouts. The problem was that the tryouts were being held before the state playoffs were over. Here's a kid and his parents who were faced with a decision of whether or not to allow the young man to tryout. The possibility of the kid getting hurt and missing the state playoffs weighed heavily on their minds. The parents eventually talked the kid out of the tryout, but why should a high school player, at a time in his or her life that should be the most exciting, even be faced with such a dilemma. As I said earlier, I'm not against AAU or traveling squads. They definitely have opened the recruiting lines to kids, who may not have gotten the exposure otherwise, but to cross the time lines of the high school season and conduct tryouts is wrong, and there needs to be a better way to accommodate those involved. There needs to be a time for high school kids to be high school kids. Would it honestly take something away from the game to allow a kid to finish his or her high school season without the stress of AAU tryouts? Has it become a "we versus them" attitude in regards to different teams and organizations? High school goes by fast enough. Those of us who look back on those years attest to the fact that the time was simply a blur. Shouldn't kids enjoy their experience? Shouldn't their four high school years be the best years of their teenage lives?

Exposure and traveling teams do not constitute all of the problems associated with high school sports today. There are a number of other outside sources at fault when it comes to putting unnecessary strain on the interscholastic game today. Perhaps the greatest peril threatening the survival of high school and junior high sports is none other than the fans who pay money to sit in the bleachers, proudly displaying their right to ridicule.

Coaches and administrators, though they too are sometimes in question, have a certain set of standards to which they must abide, be it school codes or league and state agendas. Additionally, the performance of high school referees is usually judged by a committee of their peers. Many leagues often allow high school coaches to submit a preferred list of officials that they would like to see work their games, and to scratch those that they do not want, in order to provide fairness and good sportsmanship. But nowhere in the game is there an agenda which constitutes proper decorum in regards to fan behavior. Fans answer to no one, and the result of unruly fans can lead school districts to drop certain teams from their schedules, and in some cases, lead to the demise of the athletic programs themselves. High school and youth leagues were not instituted as an avenue to relieve stress of the fans or rid the fan of his or her frustration.

Professional baseball's recent hysteria of fans attacking umpires in the middle of a game has become a topic of conversation in recent years. Fans attending professional sporting events, paying premium prices, may feel they have a right to attack, both physically and verbally, players who are being paid premium salaries. Although this practice is inexcusable and detrimental to the game, the security that is hired at professional sporting events can usually diffuse a situation before it gets too far out of control. But what happens when the same practice enters the high school field or gymnasium where security is minimal? Fans need to be made aware that the field, gym, or diamond associated with school activities is an extension of the school itself. People cannot just enter a school and walk into a history or math class and sound off on a teacher. Ever since the tragedy at Colombine, precautions have been put in place with regards to school buildings during the allotted school day. Outsiders entering most schools must be screened and buzzed into the building. Faculty, administrators, cafeteria workers, and custodians are often subject to wearing name tags, and students book bags are often not allowed outside of locker areas. But what precautions are there in regards to extra curriculars? People can walk in off the street, pay their token admission payments, and feel that they are entitled to have their way. In recent years, this freedom has all too often resulted in tragedy.

Fans must be subject to rules of behavior, especially when it comes to interscholastic and youth programs. Coaches try to instill in their players that it is a privilege, and not a right, to be a part of an interscholastic athletic team. While subjects taught in the classroom may be mandatory, participation in extra curricular activities is not. I always reminded my players that high school doesn't owe you the game. You, however, owe the school for giving you the opportunity to be its representative on the court. When you put on that school jersey with the school name across your chest, you are telling everyone in attendance that you are representing something bigger than yourself. Shouldn't the fan be subject to the same criteria?

School districts are subject to a certain set of rules, and the athletes who represent those schools are held to certain standards. If those rules offend outside interests or individuals, then these groups or individuals should direct their behavior toward some other level of athletics, not the high school or junior high school levels.

Fans need to take the time to learn the rules of the game. Many of the worst perpetrators are those who never played and have little understanding of what's going on. Coach bashing, official bashing, and player bashing has become all too commonplace. I've personally witnessed fans and, more often than not, parents, who have verbally attacked kids as they walked off the court. The belief that one kid doesn't pass the ball to their kid enough times in the course of a game has led to tirades that amount to physical attacks. These actions should not and can not be tolerated. The well being of the game, and the young people who play it, should not be subject to such unruly behavior. We must not allow fan behavior to become just another reason as to why kids are quitting the game at an alarming rate.

Since I've been out of coaching for the past few years, I thought it only right to discuss the state of the high school game with some active and recently retired coaches. Most of the coaches that I've interviewed are in agreement that the game, as well as all high school sports, is in a fragile state. Most are convinced that outside interference has greatly hampered coaching and team camaraderie. Both the men and women coaches agree that coaching high school sports has changed drastically in recent years. Coaches' actions and decisions are all too often brought to the attention of school administrators and athletic boards by disgruntled parents and fans. Most coaches admit to having had more than one meeting, often cutting into practice time, with the parents of a player and a member of the school administration. Unlisted phone numbers are commonplace among high school coaches, who do not want to take the game and especially the complaints home with them. Critics might label it as part of the job, but the fact remains that the longevity of quality high school coaches is vastly diminishing, and the game is suffering because of it.

This past summer, I had the pleasure of sitting down with a coach who is associated with a nationally renowned high school basketball program. The prestige and notoriety of the program causes it to provide two teams to represent it: one team is the national team, and the other team plays a regular league schedule. The regular team is by no means a junior varsity squad, but rather is comprised of players that may be just a step below the talent level of the national team. The coach informed me that the expectations of kids in both programs are extremely high. He believes that 100% of the kids who attend his school and are associated with the basketball program do so with one thing in mind: a basketball scholarship or better. The biggest problem, he says, is how unrealistic so many of these players are.

Way too many parents are convinced that their kid is next in line for a free ride into a Division I program. It's difficult, he admits, to watch kids that just aren't at that level, and probably never will be, and their parents believing that anything less is unacceptable. Parents need to become better educated in terms of talent level. They need to sit in on a Division 1 practice. They need to see just how good D-1 players are and then realistically assess their kids' chances. Big time college basketball today is believed to be a stepping stone to the professional level, and the odds of most kids, even at the prestigious schools, of making it to the top, are slim to say the least. Many of the athletes that do get recruited by such schools find themselves overwhelmed by the talent level that surrounds them.

There's no denying that the trickle down theory has had its impact on the high school game. I've talked about the pro game getting younger and younger, and the college game losing so many players to professional contracts. It's easy to see how the high school game is the next step in this downward pattern. Many high school programs are losing players for reasons that were unheard of twenty years ago. Just to be a member of a high school team isn't enough any more. If there isn't a future in the game, then many high school players tend to look at the whole experience, and the time spent as being wasted. If a kid isn't the star, or The Go to Guy, then what's the point?

Coaches are having a hard time fielding both J.V. and varsity teams.

Fingers can be pointed in a lot of different directions. The media is to blame for a lot of the problems. High school players have been sensationalized in recent years to the point of national attention. The hype given to a player like Lebron James, and the media attention that followed, has brought the high school game into a new light. The cover stories of national magazines, the sneaker companies waiting in the wings, the publicity and television coverage of his games has made him a household name not only among families who follow basketball but also by families who don't.

Lebron is not the only high school player who left his mark. It's common knowledge that high school athletes have their own websites. Cable interviews and media attention as well as advertising money to networks that televise games, has added to the frenzy. People tune in to see a player, not a team, with little concern over who wins the game. I'm betting that few people, even the most fervent sports trivia fanatics, could not name the top 3 high school teams in the country. The word team today seems to get lost in the euphoria, and because of it the high school game suffers. The fact that 1 in 35,000 high school players make it to the NBA doesn't seem to matter in the least. The ratings are based on the individual. The hype of projecting the kid into stardom is a media circus. The other players on the team are just along for the ride, seldom mentioned and easily forgotten. How difficult must it be to coach a team with a potential pro prospect? The coach might be the only one in the gym, come game night, who's focusing on a victory.

It's true that very few phenoms come along. The idea of entering the NBA draft right out of high school is relegated to an exclusive group, but it doesn't lessen the reality that it has taken away from the high school game as we knew it. Where will it stop? When will the rules change to accommodate that super junior who wants to pass up his senior year of high school? Never, the critics might say! That would be just too young. DON'T BELIEVE IT FOR A SECOND!

High school basketball was once such a simple game. Players played it for the love and the loyalty to their schools, their communities, and to the game itself. If a high school player was good enough to play at the next level, it was icing on the cake. College coaches recruited players without the use of scouting services or exposure camps. Although it may be a fact of life that modernization, technology, and the Internet dominate our very existence, it's sad to see how it has reached into the very core of our game and, like so many other aspects of our lives, taken some of the humanity out of it.

Many of the good high school players today have developed an attitude in direct correlation to the times. I once asked a pretty good high school junior about his plans for the off season, and I was amazed at his knowledge of college recruiting. He knew exactly the months that college coaches were allowed to attend summer camps, and he was in the process of scheduling his camps according to it. He also knew what AAU tournaments he would be playing in, and even which weekend shootouts would give him the best looks. This was a sixteen year-old kid managing his time to try to market himself as a player. I asked him where the good pickup games in the areas were played, and he had no idea. In a strange way I felt a little sorry for him. I guess it's the way the game is viewed today, and I've come to the realization that the term "old school" really must pertain to me, because I cannot and will not look at the game of basketball as a market, and I cannot and will not look at the high school player as a commodity.

Parents look at college scholarships with stars in their eyes. Coaches pride themselves in the part they played in the development of a player who is being recruited to play at the next level. I have even heard a story about an assistant high school coach who asked a player, on his own team, to sign an autograph for him just in case the kid makes it to the big time. The amount of high school kids who make it to Division I is minimal, in comparison to the number of high school players who are quitting the game for fear of not measuring up. Many high school players, to the dismay of their parents, coaches, and communities, are simply packing it in. It's becoming all too commonplace to hear high school and junior high school kids say, "I had enough" or "I no longer want it."

Where does the fault lie? Is there a place in the high school game for the average player any more? Lately, there has even been a run on parents finagling assistant coaching positions at the high school level. These are the same parents who coached their kids through little league, midget football, biddy-basketball, and youth soccer. Youth sports are one thing, but to coach on the high school level is completely different. Some high schools today allow coaches to carry a number of unpaid assistants and some head coaches hire them because they believe it's better to have people with you than against you. It is somewhat comical to go to a high school game and see more coaches sitting on the bench than players. Are these fathers really out to benefit the program, or are they there to generate playing time for their kids? How many of them will be around after their kid graduates? Do they move up the coaching ladder as their kid progresses from the freshman team to J.V. to varsity? Maybe it's a new day and age. Maybe the days of handing your kid over to a high school coach, with the belief that the coach will make a better man out of him, are gone.

I personally had the great fortune to play for a high school coach who demanded discipline and ran a program that players and parents were proud to be associated with. Dave Linchorst was one of those rare individuals who had a way of getting the most out of every kid on his team. Some graduates of his program swear that he could scare you into winning. Others believe that his hatred of losing made him drive his players harder than most coaches. Regardless of his motives, most fathers wanted their sons to play for him, knowing that the lessons they would learn at his feet would last a lifetime. I can only imagine a father trying to find a way into his personal domain. Dave, as well as other coaches of his era, have been labeled dinosaurs, not because of their age, but because of their approach to the game. High school coaches at one time had to pay their dues, to learn the game, to understand its importance, and to make a commitment to the game and to the players that they would coach. I'm convinced that some of these dinosaurs must shake their heads when they see how outside interferences have found a way into their game.

Do parents realize the damage they may be doing? Kids need to understand that the Team is the most important element when it comes to high school athletics, not the amount of individual playing time. Is there still value on contributing for the sake of the team, or is the team concept being phased out completely? Those of us who still attend high school games and cheer for our favorite teams truly hope not, but are we becoming more and more of a minority in the scheme of high school basketball?

Some believe that the game has evolved to the point where amateurism is a farce. Payments that are being made to players, in the form of equipment or spending money, are a reality. Arguments over whether or not a college scholarship is a cheap way for schools to capitalize on a student athlete's income-based-potential are common among sports talk show hosts. Is the ongoing frenzy associated with players like LeBron James a further breakdown of amateurism, and how low, in terms of grade level, it can go? Will the rules someday change to allow a high school junior to opt out his senior year and declare himself eligible for the draft? Of course, the powers that be say it will never happen, but what will they say when LeBron II comes along? What will the hype be for that "sixteen year old phenom" who's wasting his time in high school? How long will the sneaker companies, endorsement giants, and cable TV stations wait? The argument will be that the kid is an exception, that rare talent that comes along once in a lifetime and must be nurtured. How can we justify holding him back when he's marketable now? He'll be a first round draft pick and make millions, or maybe by that time billions. Who are we to hold him back?

Does it all sound familiar? Haven't we heard it all before? True, it's just that one kid, but how does it affect the millions of high school players whose dreams have now been shot down by another year? How far down the basketball chain will it show its ugly hand? How many parents of those third and fourth graders will succumb to the belief that maybe their kid is next in line? What will happen when they come to the realization that their child is not the diamond in the rough? Will the game suffer once again by kids quitting long before they ever really had a chance to fall in love with the game? And, even more important, will the child suffer in terms of lost self-esteem and confidence, that he or she never had the opportunity to develop at such a fragile age? When will it all stop? When will the powers finally say, "That's Enough?" When will high school proms and pep rallies get back to being the most important part of a sixteen-year-olds life? I'm sorry to say, "Probably Never"!

I recently had the pleasure of attending a fall pep rally in one of our local high schools. My hat goes off to the athletic director who addressed the gym, full of parents and fans that came out to show their support. She started out by congratulating all the athletes, band members, and coaches in attendance and wished them all good luck. She then went on to emphasize the importance of camaraderie among the members of the high school community, and how vital it was to take pride in being a member of a team. She told the students and everyone present that the only opponents that we should face during the course of the year are the teams wearing the different color uniforms. She placed great emphasis on the fact that schools cannot get caught up in competing against members of our own team for if that is allowed to happen the whole team concept will be damaged. I truly hope that her message got through to the right people, although, I believe, many turned a deaf ear. Kids today need to know the importance of the team. They need to understand the value that each one contributes to the common goal, and the fact that whether they win or lose, they did it together. There's no denying that there will be enough individual pressure facing them later in life, when the ultimate "ME" takes over, but it doesn't have to start at such an early age, and it doesn't have to infect a group of individuals whose friendships should greatly outweigh their "future careers". Kids are not born with a selfish attitude; it is instilled in them by adults who claim to be looking out for their best interests.

Perhaps the greatest award that I have ever received, and one of my most treasured possessions, was given to me by one of my former teams made up of some outstanding young men. It's a picture of a group of people's hands put together, as if they were about to break a huddle and head onto the court. Upon close observation, you notice that they are the hands of both men and women of different color. Some of the hands protrude from suit coats, some from flannel shirts and some from expensive blouses. The caption at the bottom of the poster size picture reads:

TEAMWORK

"NEVER DOUBT THAT A SMALL GROUP
OF THOUGHTFUL, COMMITTED, PEOPLE

CAN CHANGE THE WORLD.
INDEED, IT'S THE ONLY THING
THAT EVER HAS."

I proudly display this poster in my recreation room, and I always dwell on its message while talking to groups that are working toward a common goal. I constantly remind my students of the power associated with it, and I know that if the urge would ever come over me to go back into the coaching ranks, it would be at the very core of my program.

# No Names

When I make reference to the No-Names, it is by no means a derogatory slur. On the contrary, the no-names are the truest basketball people I know. These are the players who play the game, and always did, out of pure love for the sport. Most of them played high school basketball, but few progressed to the next level. Some attended college and made a career out of the intramural programs. Others went to work, but made sure that their work schedules or shifts co-existed with the pickup games and summer leagues that dominated most of their free time. I'm sure that every town and city across the country has a few of these "Hoop Heads". They are the guys who covet their keys to the local gyms. They're the ones to call when you're looking for a meaningful workout or pickup game. They're the ones that the good high school coaches tell their players to look up if they want to get better in the off season. And you can rest assured that if there is a good game going on in your town, and the best players are playing; they will always be found in the middle of it. They go by names like Rock, Murph, and the Eggman, and if you ask any of them why they played the game well into their forties or even fifties, they'll all give you the same answer, "Because it's the greatest game in the world."

These are the players I knew would tell it like it is. They played in countless pickup games and recreation leagues over the past three decades. Some are still playing, though every year seems to take its toll. Some have done stints as coaches, and others have gotten into officiating. A few have gracefully unlaced the sneakers and succumbed to Father Time, but in all my years around the game, none comes close to their understanding and passion for the game they love. I knew that if this book would ever become a reality, I would have to sit down with a few of these warriors. I knew that I would have to get their reaction with respect to the game and how it has changed over the years. I must admit that the time that I spent with these guys, and the enthusiasm they provided, might have been the most enjoyable hours spent on this endeavor.

On a cool fall afternoon in November, I sat down with two of these No-Names, in what was once the vestibule of an old church in the town where I grew up. Bob "Eggy" Killian bought the old church and is renovating it into a house for himself and his wife. Bob is forty-five years old and has lived in Mahanoy City, Pa. his entire life. Eggy, as he's known to all of his friends, is a basketball fanatic. He was a fixture in the playground throughout his youth, and he went on to an outstanding high school career. He also goes down, in the annals of the school yard, as one of its greatest trash talkers. Eggy recalls how obsessed he was with the game when he was growing up. He remembers once missing a foul shot in a high school game and being so upset, he decided to get up early every morning before school to shoot fouls at the playground. After about a week, he remembers the priest coming out and telling him that he wouldn't be able to continue his ritual. It seems the people of the neighborhood were complaining that the ball bouncing at 6:00 a.m. was constantly waking them up.

Upon graduating from high school, Eggy pursued a degree in education and is presently a middle school science teacher at his alma mater. Over the years he's served as both a basketball and football coach and is presently the high school golf coach. He admits, in today's world, coaching golf is great since there are no parents and no referees.

Eggy played in pickup games every Thursday night and Saturday afternoon well into his thirties, and he insists that everything that he has accomplished in his life can, in some way, be tied to the game of basketball. "I've learned the value of teamwork, of friendship, of competition, and more than anything, I've learned persistence. I was never blessed with great natural ability, but I always believed that I could outwork anyone. I also learned to place great value of punctuality. Unlike some of the other kids growing up in my neighborhood, I had to work with my Dad, a carpenter, from the time I was in sixth grade. Free time to me was cherished, and I spent all of it in the playground. I always remember that the good games on the weekends would start at 1:00 p.m., and if you were late you didn't get picked." Eggy claims that he never missed the choosing of teams. "I'd make sure that I would be at the playground no later than 12:30. To this day, my wife cannot understand why I'm always on time for everything. I can't comprehend how people can be constantly late, and I know I can trace my obsession with punctuality back to those Saturday afternoon pickup games."

Eggy stresses that, by far, the greatest lesson he learned through the game of basketball is the belief that he can accomplish anything he puts his mind to. Admitting that he was not the most gifted student in high school, he knew, deep down, that he would get a college education simply because some of his teachers said he would never make it. Now that he is teaching alongside the very teachers who doubted his ability, he simply smiles and emphatically states, "They were wrong about the Eggman."

Hard work and the will to take on any challenge still dominate Eggy's life. A few years back he single handedly built a miniature golf course. He moved 40,000 large rocks from a mountain to his site as well as transported 100 tons of crushed stone by wheel barrel. When deciding to take on his latest project of transforming this old church into his permanent dwelling, once again, many people considered it a foolish undertaking. Many asked him, "Why not just build a new house?" "It's always the doubt, the skepticism of others that inspires me. It's that competitive attitude, the will to succeed that I never seem to grow out of. Eggy and his wife plan on moving into the house within the year and he laughs about some of the critics who told him he was crazy for taking on the task, since now they are referring to him as a genius.

The game of basketball was not only important to those of us who played it a generation ago, it was also cherished by some that just loved being around it. Eggy and I laughed about a summer league that we played in many years ago. There was an older fellow from our hometown that was one of those sports junkies, and all the guys on our summer league team knew him. After winning the league championship on a hot summer night we proceeded to our favorite watering hole. About an hour after our arrival, one of our teammates, who left a little earlier and now returned, informed us that the old guy was just arrested by the police. We later learned that he was trying to break the window of a local jewelry store. When questioned by the police about his actions, he tried to impress upon the officer that he was only trying to get some watches for his favorite team, since they just won the summer league championship. I don't recall charges ever being brought against him, but it does go down as one the great stories of our basketball past.

Scott Hudson is thirty-seven years old; he is the

ultimate gym rat. He was the starting point guard, as a senior, for his high school team and has been playing the position in adult leagues for the past eighteen years. "Rocky" takes pride in the fact that his adult league team is still comprised of some of his old high school teammates. When I asked him what it is that keeps him playing, he answers simply, "I just can't imagine my life without playing the game. There's nothing greater than being able to get together with old friends and play the game that ultimately brought us together in the first place." He professes that many of the young players today just don't understand that there's more to the game than just going out to see how many points you can score in a summer league game. A lot of the young players have this chip on their shoulder that me versus you attitude. They don't seem to enjoy the game, and they have little respect for the older guys who they often come up against in these leagues. Rocky believes that his team usually does well because, "We simply enjoy playing together. With us, it doesn't matter who scores and who doesn't. No one keeps stats. We just like being out there playing, and I find it strange that others can't see the simplicity in it." It bothers me, he confesses, even in pickup games, when young players sound off. "I remember growing up in the playground, and the great feeling you'd get when an older guy would give you a high five or maybe even pulled you aside to offer you some advice."

Rocky stands about 5'7" tall and weighs in at about

130lbs. soaking wet, but his size never deterred his passion for the game. "Being as small as I was, the desire to get picked into the playground games, when I was younger, was a major challenge. I realized early on that if I could find a way to keep other players happy that they would pick me in the Prime Time games. I've learned that passing the basketball can be much more rewarding than scoring. Everyone wants to score, but if you love to pass then all the scorers want you on their team."

Like Eggy, Scott remembers the importance placed on playground punctuality. He jokingly remembers two brothers who were constantly late. They lived about two blocks from the court, and they would always send their younger brother screaming down the street proclaiming that they were on their way and to pick them in. He also laughs reminiscing about one Sunday afternoon, many years ago, when a group of guys from another town pulled up to the playground in their cars looking for a game. When the game began the visitors set up in a 2-3 zone defense. Scott remembers one of the players from the home team stopping the game and informing the newcomers that no one plays zone in this playground. He told them that if the priest from the rectory comes out and sees them in a zone, he'll kick us all out and close down the court.

Aside from playing, Scott works for the postal system and is the freshman basketball coach at his alma mater. "I love coaching", Scott admits. "It allows me the chance to teach kids, not only the game, but also the many positives that go along with it. I try to instill in them a love for it. I don't get too wrapped up in wins and losses. It's much more important to develop a respect for the game and for the players that they play with and against. I'm constantly reminding them that the guys they're competing against now will become friends of theirs in the future, if they continue playing."

Rocky Hudson epitomizes everything that's right with the game today, and I only hope he continues coaching, for the profession needs more guys like him. Though the certainty of his longevity as a coach may be suspect, one thing is certain. Come summer time, he and his former playing-mates will, once again, regroup and enter whatever town decides to sponsor a summer league because as Rocky put it, "I just can't imagine my life without the game."

In 1976, I was hired as a Social Studies Teacher and Head Boys Basketball Coach at Minersville Areas High School in Minersville, Pa. On my initial visit to the town, I drove by a playground adjoined to the football field and stopped to watch some kids playing pickup, thinking that maybe a few of them might be members of my upcoming team. As I sat in my car with the windows down observing the action, I was startled by a tap on my shoulder. The man who greeted me that summer morning was Bill Murphy, and though I didn't realize it at the time, I was in the presence of guy with whom, over the next fifteen years,

I would spend countless hours playing the game we loved.

Murph is a basketball legend in Minersville. He led his 1966 high school team to twenty-two straight wins and was regarded by coaches and players alike as one of the best players in the entire region. Upon graduation Murph entered the workforce and started on a basketball career that would take him to just about every gym and playground within a fifty-mile radius, some even further. Murph remembers playing semi-pro ball for a local team and traveling to Maryland where he once played against a pretty good big man by the name of John Thompson. For more than thirty years Murph played in every summer league, recreation league, double elimination tournament, and pickup game that he could find. He laughs when he talks about always carrying his gym bag in the back of his car just in case he might stumble across a playground with a game in progress. Murph, like all the great gym rats, was the guy to call if you were looking for a game. It was not uncommon for a high school kid, twenty years his junior, to receive a call from Murph regarding a pickup game that needed a body. Some of the parents of those kids who went to school with Murph and knew him best would tell their son, "You better get your butt up to the gym. Murph called, and they need a player".

Murph remembers growing up with the game. He talks about always wanting to get better. "I'd do anything to improve. If someone said you need to get stronger, I'd lift weights; I'd shoot jumpers and play shooting games constantly to improve my shot. I even used to go up to the football stadium and stand under the bleachers and jump up to touch the bottom side of the steps, thinking that I could improve my jumping ability by graduating from one step to the next." Murph smiles as he reminisces about the days when he'd play three or four hours a day at the playground. He says, "It's funny, but I can still remember the smells associated with the different jerseys that I'd wear. There was just no better feeling than the exhaustion that accompanied a successful day on the courts." Murph, like so many other players from a generation past, feels sorry for today's young players, who tend to look at the game in a different light. "I often drive by playgrounds that twenty to thirty years ago were packed with kids, only to find them idle. I just don't believe kids love it as much. Priorities have changed. Life has become too complicated.

Murph and I have been friends for more than twenty years. When we sat down recently to talk we couldn't help but reminisce about the times we spent playing the game. He jogged my memory about a Friday evening, many years ago, when the two of us were working out in a small elementary gym. After about a dozen games of *HORSE* we began playing one-on-one full court. At the time there was a college kid, a starting running back for a Division 1 college program, who happened to be lifting weights in the adjoining weight room. He heard the ball bouncing and walked over to the gym only to find the two of us running up and down the court in the heat of battle. As we exited the gym he stopped us, a little confused as to why two guys in their thirties would be spending a Friday night going at it as hard as we were. Murph asked me if I remembered the two of us laughing at the kid's dilemma. Murph also reminded me of a night, after playing a number of pickup games; we stopped by a local pub for a few beers and witnessed Reggie Jackson hitting three home runs in a World Series Game. It often amazes me how the game can jog one's memory.

Today, in his late fifties, Bill Murphy is still involved with the game he loves. Though he doesn't play quite as much any more, mainly due to an operation on a spinal tumor ten years back, he continues to get up and down the court as a high school and college official, a hobby that started twenty-six years ago. He also contends, "I haven't given up entirely on playing. I still like to show up at the gym when the high school kids are around and get into a little half court action with them." I only hope that the kids know who the guy with the gray hair is and I pray that some of these kids will take with them a little of the passion that Murph put into the game for more than half a century.

Every town, every playground, every school yard that cultivated players a generation ago can boast of its greatest players. Arguments and comparisons can and will be made as to who were the best players. Legends tend to get larger and larger as the years go by, but one thing is for sure, basketball, the true meaning of it, can only be understood by those who wrapped their lives around it.

Someone once made the statement that there are two types of peoples associated with the game of basketball: those who play basketball and basketball players. The real No-Names are the truest form of basketball players that you'll ever find. They don't need crowds, referees, stat sheets, or uniforms. Give them access to a gym where they can lace up the sneakers two or three times a week and you'll see basketball at its best. I urge fathers who have kids that want to be players to find out where the old guys play and take your sons or daughters to watch. Tell them to study the faces, to see the determination, and to watch the little things that they do. Have them talk to some of these veterans about how great the game is. No better lesson will they ever receive.

My hat goes off to all of you "No Namers" out there. You know who you are and you exemplify the game better than anyone ever will. I wish that the powers that be could only take a look at the game through the eyes of those who truly played it like so many did in the past. Maybe the bottom line could be erased just a little bit. Maybe the smell of the gym or the sound of the ball could once again become the driving force behind a game that once was so simple yet so important.

# SUCCESS

# SUCCESS

They said to be successful
In everything you do
Succeed in all your schoolwork
Be the best as you go through

Be successful in your business
Make money while you can
Be successful, be a leader
Be respected, be a man

For success is so important
It determines how you'll live
And success is what to strive for
It's the measure that you give

So we live to be successful
with its pressures and it's stress
But we never take the time to ask
What's the meaning of success?

Is it really so important
To get everything you can
To be the best, the top, the king
In short to be "The Man"

Could success not be so final,
But a journey that we take
Could the journey have some failures
and some losses, and bad breaks

Could success be something special
That's not measured by just wealth
Could success have much more substance
Based on love, and faith, and health

I like to think success can be
So simple in a way.
If we're thankful for the things we have
Then success comes every day

—dah

Perhaps the greatest concern facing members of the younger generation is their ability to measure up or not measure up to what society perceives as success. For some unknown reason, we have fostered the belief that success is solely measured in terms of wins, high grades, huge salaries, fancy cars, houses with swimming pools, and extensive wardrobes. As adults, we tend to forget what it was like to be young, having to live up to expectations that others held before us. We constantly pressure young people today to conform to our adult ways of thinking. We look at education solely based on grades, class rank, SAT scores, and too often, kids who do not live up to our specification are considered unsuccessful. Falling short of the requirements to get into a particular school, being cut from a team, receiving second or third honors as opposed to first is not the measure on which future lives will be judged. Unrealistic goals and out of reach standards society deems important has not driven every child to try harder. Some kids today simply give up. Many consider themselves unsuccessful at a very early age for fear of failure. Many kids choose not to get involved in extra curricular activities that can broaden their horizons because of this fear. Success, for many, has become so far out of reach that they simply stop trying. The feeling that they can never do enough, or can never live up to expectations, has too often added to the generation gap and rightly so.

Adults need to become realists. We need to encourage this generation to do their best and be the best that they can be while not always comparing them to others. We need to remember the uniqueness of the individual and take it from there. The kid who's five feet tall and weighs in at 125 pounds is not going to make it in the NFL, no matter how hard he works, but that does not mean he shouldn't work hard. Some students, no matter how hard they study, will not bring home the perfect report card. To "be the best you can be" is often not enough in the eyes of those who want you to be more. By no means am I negating the results that can be achieved and often overachieved through hard work and discipline, but sometimes we lose perspective as to the goals that might be achieved through it.

Parents are quick to examine box-scores. They count their kids' points and they constantly critique every missed shot and turnover, reminding the youngster that such play will definitely hurt their chances for playing at the next level, whatever level that may be. How many of these parents ever take the time to ask their kids if they even want to play at the next level? Most kids, I'm betting, could care less about their future playing status and they shouldn't. Parents need to put themselves in their kid's shoes. They need to try to remember what life was like as a teenager and to help them along. Far too many adults today have a tendency to forget about the learning process that includes disappointments, failures, rejections, and the everyday ups and downs that go along with being a teenager. One of the most damaging problems facing this evolving generation is the bottom line mentality that is constantly drummed into them. Does everything have to have a final outcome? Must there always be a comparative study on every aspect of their lives? Must they succeed at all cost?

The word "success" is the most misunderstood and misdirected word in the English language. The idea of the final result or the ultimate ending is incomprehensible. Whenever I'm in the company of a group of people and the mention of someone's success pops up, be it a coach, a player, or a person in the business world, I tell them to imagine a team that has a perfect record, an undefeated season—24 and 0. I then tell them to imagine the team from the next town over, in the same league, who is 0 and 24, winless the entire season. It's easy for them to choose the team with the greatest success. I then ask them to imagine the very next season when both teams compile identical records of 12 and 12, winning and losing half of their games. I ask the group to judge the team that has the greatest success now. Most agree that the team that came from the 0 and 24 mark to a 500 record is much more successful and, according to today's standards, they may be right. The coach of that team will definitely get hired back for next season, and the program will take on the label of heading in the right direction. On the other hand, the team that went from 24 and 0 to the 500 mark will be judged as not living up to expectations. The coach will no doubt be on thin ice and told that he better get the program back where it belongs. These are two completely different teams in a different season, but the roots of success have been drawn, no matter how unfairly, on what each team did a year back. Does ending with a favorable result always constitute success?

Does winning every game or does getting an *A* in every class guarantee your success in life? I'm sorry if I seem to be a skeptic, but I don't believe success is an ending. Success is merely a step in the right direction in an ongoing journey through life, a journey that starts when we take that first step and continues throughout our lives, coming to a close only when we take that final breath.

A few years ago, I was asked to speak at a High School girl's basketball banquet. The team that I was to speak to had just completed a remarkable season, finishing with a record of 32 wins and 0 losses and winning a state championship. Three of the girls on the team were 1,000 point scorers and preparing to take their talents to the next level to compete on the college scene. This was a team that most coaches only dream about. They were fast, smart, dedicated, and determined to do something great, and they disappointed no one. I must admit that, although I've spoken at other sports affairs, this one was a little special, based on their accomplishments.

On my drive to the banquet I found myself lost in thought about how great a season they had. I considered all of the awards that they would receive individually and as a team. I couldn't help but think about all of the people that would be present, the proud parents who would be in attendance and the coaches who would look at this team for the last time, and remember all of the little things that they went through together. I thought of the girls themselves sitting together, heads held a little higher, knowing that they were going to be the center of attention.

I started to consider my congratulatory remarks, which would include the Coach of the Year, The Player of the Year, to the League, District, and State Champions, and I guess I didn't comprehend the magnitude of the evening until I arrived at the banquet. As I entered the hall I was taken back by the spectacle. A State Championship banner hung behind the speakers table, with trophies and plaques of all shapes and sizes, and presents piled on each of the tables. The girls were decked out, parents were shaking hands, and tears and hugs started from the get go. I knew that this was going to be a very special night.

I learned from my father, whose hobby was public speaking, to always start off with a humorous story. He said that it sets the tone for your message, focuses attention, and lightens the mood, and more than anything else, relaxes the speaker. I told the girls a story that happened to me a few years back when I was coaching high school boys. We were preparing to play a game against the boy's team from their school—I neglected to say that the team that I was addressing was a Catholic High School and the reason I'm bringing this up now is that it fits into my story. The coach of the team was a very good friend of mine by the name of Tim Coyle. I told the girls that there was a certain mystique about playing against their school. I proceeded by translating a dream that startled me the night prior to the game.

I told them that in my dream the Angel Gabrielle

appeared to me and took me up to heaven. As he walked me through the Pearly Gates people began to walk up to me with hands extended in a genuine gesture of friendship. They all welcomed me and began to congratulate me for reasons I did not know. After about an hour of walking and shaking hands, we descended into a beautiful little valley and at the bottom of the valley, painted into a scenic background, stood a little cottage with a white picket fence. There was a little stream flowing next to the house, and the entire picture was surrounded by flowers and blooming trees. As we got closer I noticed that from each window and doorway there were flags and banners flying, and on each one was the name of my school and a picture of our mascot. I was a bit dumbfounded as I looked at the angel for some clarification, and, sporting a smile, he told me that he had a special surprise for me.

At that point I saw a magnificent light descend upon us and the Good Lord Himself appeared—talk about being in the presence of greatness. The Lord presented Himself directly in front of me and said "Coach, for all of your work with the youth of America, and for all the time that you put into helping young people you are about to receive a very special award." He went on to say that He does not bestow this award on just anyone. He pointed in the direction of the cottage and then said, "This beautiful cottage is going to be your home for all eternity." Needless to say, I was taken back by the entire spectacle; however, as the Good

Lord was speaking, my eyes began to wander to the top of the mountain surrounding my valley. There I noticed a huge, white mansion. This splendid building had great marble pillars and statues surrounding it, and as I looked a little closer I noticed that there were huge banners and pennants, the color of the Catholic school that we were preparing to play, extending from every window. It was such a magnificent work of architecture that it took my breath away. When I regained my composure, I sheepishly said to the Lord, please don't take this the wrong way or think that I am ungrateful, but I have to ask you a question. Pointing to the mansion with the school banners swaying in the breeze, I asked, "What did Coach Coyle do throughout his life to warrant such a magnificent home?" The Good Lord looked at me a little surprised and then began to laugh, hysterically. "That home is not Coach Coyle's," he reiterated, "It's Mine!"

Now that I broke the ice and eased the tension, especially on myself, it was time to get to the main reason I was here. I started out by congratulating this very special team, the coaches, managers, athletic director, and everyone else who played a part in their extraordinary season. I praised their commitment and their accomplishments, putting great emphasis on this last word. I told the girls that I always use the word accomplishment because I believe that the word success is the worst word in the English language. The dictionary defines success as, "a favorable result or ending, the gaining of wealth, position, and fame." I asked the girls to think about some of the famous people who have achieved great wealth and fame. Many of these people have suffered through personal crises in their every day lives. Many have made the covers of supermarket tabloids and are prominent guests at posh rehabilitation centers and mental clinics. Many have police records and personal problems that follow them constantly. Many simply cannot handle the demands that go along with stardom.

I asked the girls how they would have felt if they lost the last game of the season. Would they consider themselves unsuccessful? I told them that I had the great pleasure of seeing them play on a number of occasions, and I believe that, even if they didn't finish perfect, to me they were great because of the drive and tenacity they played with for thirty two minutes each and every time they took the floor. I told them, to me that was success.

The thought of success being a favorable result or ending is utterly ridiculous in terms of human endeavors. What happens when you reach a favorable result or ending? Are you no longer successful? I asked the girls, "Now that your season has come to a close, and you walked away with a championship, are you no longer successful?" I reiterated that, as a team, they were great achievers, but they were not successful for success is never final.

Delving into my social studies teaching background, I proceeded to tell them a story that happened years ago as the Great Depression was finally coming to an end. There was a meeting scheduled by our national leaders, comprised of the greatest economic minds of the day. There were a few millionaire business leaders in the group, a member of the national government's economic team, and a few others representing the top stock commissions from around our country. The goal of the meeting was to study the problems that led to the economic collapse and to comprise a plan that would prevent such an economic disaster from ever happening again. These were, without a doubt, the most notable economic minds of our society, great "successes" in their life's work.

I told the girls that, within five years of that important meeting, two of the men who attended had filed for bankruptcy, two others committed suicide, and another was committed to a mental hospital after suffering a nervous breakdown. I re-emphasized that success is not based on the amount of money that one earns, it's not determined by one's fame or popularity, and it's not based on the amount of rebounds or points accumulated in one's career. Success is a "journey". It's an excursion through life that will be filled with ups and downs, accomplishments and disappointments, good times and bad times, and achievements and failures. The key to success, I told them, is the ability to keep moving forward. To take on the many challenges of life, knowing that everything is not always going to be as perfect as it is tonight. I told them that the best way to envision success is to think in terms of mountains and valleys, "Tonight you're all standing on top of the mountain. Enjoy it, cherish it, but do not believe that it will last forever because the valleys are up ahead. Do not be afraid of the valleys because they are an important part of life and they will make you stronger."

I singled out the girls who were facing graduation and wandering what the future would hold in store for them. Where would they be a year from tonight? I wished them luck, and instructed them to face each new challenge with the kind of integrity that they faced every opponent during the season. To the returning underclass girls, I told them to get prepared because next season is right around the corner and they'll be starting all over again. Expectations for them will be high, and new challenges will be facing them as a completely different team. I wished them all health and happiness, and then informed then that it was time for me to close, and in doing so I would like to give them my definition of success. I told them that to me, success is defined in two simple words, "WHAT'S NEXT".

# SUCCESS

To laugh often and much to win
the respect of intelligent people
and the affection of children;
to earn the appreciation of honest
critics and endure the betrayal of
false friends; to appreciate beauty,
to find the best in others;
to leave the world a bit better, whether
by a healthy child, a garden patch
or a redeemed social condition;
to know even one life has breathed
easier because you have lived,
That is to have succeeded

—Ralph Waldo Emerson

# MOTIVATION

Motivation, the ability to move someone to effort or action, seems to be a popular topic in today's world. Motivators are contracted to deliver inspiring messages to corporate groups. The keynote speakers at national conventions, dealing with everything from food preparation to electrical equipment to computer technology, are often the authors of motivational literature that head the best seller lists. Teachers, administrators, managers, and corporate employees attend conferences and workshops on motivation, and are often asked to present programs to their colleagues.

Why are millions spent to rejuvenate and revitalize today's attitude toward the workplace? Why do Fortune 500 companies deem it so important to motivate their employees? Could it be that the average person today needs that extra push? Could it be the stress associated with our jobs needs to be countered with a purpose? Does the job market today reflect our society needing some incentive, aside from a paycheck, to be the best that we can be? Or simply, can the love of a sport motivate us and project us beyond our capabilities?

I personally like motivational speakers. I guess it's the athlete in me that gets excited, and feels the juices flowing whenever I hear a rousing narrative. Over the past few years I've had the opportunity to listen to some outstanding motivators. My wife, for many years attended a national conference associated with her job and I've tagged along to several of them. She is employed as the Director of Business and Finance for one of the campuses of a major university. Since the focus is college, many of the speakers have educational directives that I've found beneficial to my work as a teacher.

I've found that my favorite part of the conferences has been the keynote speakers that are brought in to start off the festivities. Most are renowned motivators who have the ability to deliver awe inspiring messages, and I must confess that seldom have I been disappointed. Though I've heard quite a few, my favorite was a man by the name of Desi Williamson. I first heard him speak at a convention held in San Juan, Puerto Rico, and I was enthralled by his enthusiasm. Desi took the stage early in the morning and within minutes he was able to turn a tired Caribbean crowd into an excited group. Desi spoke for better than two hours and in that time he never stopped moving around the stage. He told stories of his childhood, growing up in a tough inner city neighborhood. He talked about his family and the problems he faced growing up as an African-American city kid from a split home. Desi talked about the people in his life who cared for him and gave him direction and how the game of football became his way out. He spoke about how his drive to become an athlete taught him to drive himself in every aspect in his life. He told us about his personal challenges and how every person is compelled to deal with their own struggles. He talked about working for a number of the Fortune 500 companies but not without some setbacks and disappointments, and he told the crowd about certain people and events that motivated him along his journey.

He talked about being inspired by the story of Branch Ricky, the owner of the old Brooklyn Dodgers, who was sickened by the hate and prejudice in Major League Baseball. He explained how Ricky went out and signed, against popular opinion, a young African-American by the name of Jackie Robinson to play for his team. He discussed how Ricky impressed on Robinson the difficulties he would face, not only from opposing players and fans but maybe even from his own teammates, and he explained how Robinson, no matter how bad the insults and no matter how bad he would be sabotaged, would never be able to fight back. Ricky continually reminded Robinson that his play on the field would be his only means of retaliation. Desi Williamson told a crowd of 300 plus on that hot summer morning that Branch Ricky, a white man, and Jackie Robinson, a black man, not only changed the Brooklyn Dodgers but changed the American pastime, due to their motivational convictions.

Desi also talked about another story from the world of sports that inspired and motivated him. He told the story of Roger Bannister, who accomplished the unthinkable and the impossible by breaking the four minute mile, and how thirty seven others would later achieve this feat because of a stronger conviction instilled in them by Bannister. He also talked about the commitment and determination of men from the field of sports like Jim Brown and Walter Payton, and the effect of their inspiration on so many by the way they played the game of football with such passion.

Away from sports, he talked about people who paid a price so that our lives and the lives of our children can run a little smoother. The commitment of people like Mahatma Ghandi, Mother Theresa, and Martin Luther King should be an inspiration to us all.

I can honestly say that I could have sat and listened to Desi Williamson for a few more hours that day. I can't speak for the others in attendance that morning, but for me it was well worth getting up a little earlier. Great motivational speakers and writers to can do that, they can make your day and give you a better perspective on life. They can put a smile on your face and a tear in your eye and make you realize how fortunate you are to simply be alive.

Another outstanding motivational speaker that I've had the great privilege to witness is Dan Clark. Dan is the co-author of many of the *Chicken Soup for the Soul,* books. If you haven't taken the time, I urge everyone to read this wonderful series of short stories that encompass topics from *Chicken Soup for the Teenage Soul,* to *Chicken Soup for the Pet Lovers,* to Chicken Soup for Just About Everything. I promise that it will do your heart and mind well to set aside some time to enjoy a number of these fine stories.

I heard Dan Clark speak at a convention in Las Vegas. He was the keynote speaker that tipped off the convention, and he was simply outstanding. Like Desi Williamson, Dan was a former college football player. He told a story of how his football career came to an end with a very serious injury, one that most doctors believed would leave him with permanent paralysis. Dan talked about his drive, and his will to overcome his physical setbacks, and though given little chance by the experts, defied the odds by never giving up. Today Dan is fully recovered and is a songwriter, author, and motivational speaker. His message, one that I have since used in many of my talks with young people, is one of faith and determination, and the belief that the mind can overcome more than imaginable.

I guess the reason these two individuals motivated me more than others might have to do with their attributing so much of their achievements to the lessons they learned through sports. The world of sports has always been a building block for rousing, inspirational, stories. For example, Lou Gehrig's speech at Yankee Stadium after being diagnosed with the deadly ALS disease, when he told the New York fans, "Today, I consider myself the luckiest man on the face of the earth", or Knute Rockney's, "Win one for the Gipper", has inspired athletes across generations. My personal, favorite inspirational story is that of Glenn Cunningham, the great miler of the 1930's. At the age of five, Cunningham was seriously burned in a fire and was told by the doctors who examined him that he would never walk again. He was told, at this young age, to prepare himself for a life restricted to a wheelchair. Glenn refused to accept the diagnosis and swore that he would one day walk again. His determination, though he suffered through excruciating pain, led him to a rehabilitation program that started with simply dragging himself to his feet and eventually standing without the aid of crutches or braces. After conquering these initial goals, Glenn set his sights higher. He taught himself how to walk again and then he began to run, slowly at first but then with a little more purpose. In 1934, this extraordinary young man set the world record in the mile and was later honored as the Outstanding Athlete of a Century.

There are countless motivational movies out their today. A browse through your local video store can produce a heartwarming story that has the power to lift you out of your seat and get your juices flowing. Every coach seems to have their favorite films. *Rudy, Remember the Titans*, and *Hoosiers* have been given special places in most coaches' video libraries. Although it's not a movie about sports, the movie that inspires me is the 1960 film *Spartacus.* For those of you who are too young to remember this epic starring Kirk Douglas and Jean Simmons, it's the story of a Roman slave who, together with other slaves, escapes from a gladiator school and leads a rebellion that sets fear into the garrison of Rome. It's one of the great underdog stories of all time.

When I was coaching, I would always require my players to stay after practice, either during Thanksgiving or Christmas break, to watch the movie. I'd have my assistant coach order some sandwiches and sodas, and we'd leave the game out on the court and go back in time with Spartacus for a few hours. My players always seemed to enjoy the movie and I would always stop and replay the speech that Spartacus made to his men prior to leading them into their final battle, a battle that he knew they couldn't win. As he stood on the top of a hill overlooking his followers, he reminded them that they traveled a long way together, fought many battles and won great victories and he told them that instead of taking ship for our homes across the sea that they would have to fight again. He finished his speech by reminding his men that they were brothers and that they were free. Even though Spartacus was not a movie about sports the message of brotherhood and camaraderie is loud and clear.

Many people believe that coaching is synonymous with motivation. Coaches can motivate players but only if players learn to motivate themselves first. I never believed that it was the coach's job to motivate. If a player can walk into a gymnasium or onto a playing field on game night and not be excited about the contest then how can the words of another individual make a meaningful difference? I think some coaches are great speakers prior to a game because they are so motivated themselves. They get themselves so worked up and, knowing they cannot play the game themselves, release their inhibitions on the team before leaving the confines of the locker room.

The greatest form of motivation comes through example. Parents, teachers, bosses, coaches, and speakers all set examples that can be viewed by others. The player that is the first one to practice every day and the last one to leave may be ridiculed by some but not by those who aspire to do great things. The human interest story, the one who overcomes hardship, the never say die attitude, and the ability to go on when everything and everyone around convinces you to quit, these are the motivators, and in the field of sport there are many.

Far too many of today's athletes, I'm sorry to say, are not motivated by inspirational stories, and great athletic achievements as much as they are by rewards. Don't get me wrong, I'm not against the benefits earned through hard work, but the greatest reward should be the gratification one feels for a job well done. The satisfaction of knowing you went above and beyond your capabilities to accomplish something should far outweigh the material rewards one may receive. Whether we want to admit it or not, we live in a society where shortcuts are the accepted norm. People constantly search for the easy way out. The motivational factor that dominates a substantial amount of our time is often channeled into the practice of finding a way to beat the system. Motivation should first come out of a commitment. Whatever we involve ourselves in, be it a sport or an activity, school or the workplace, relationships or simply family life, we should attack it with a passion. Only through a deep commitment can we truly be motivated.

If you love to play a sport, you'll enjoy working at it, and the more you work at it the better you'll become. If you enjoy school, the more you'll work at it; the better you be at it. There's no secret or motivational magic behind it. I use the word "work" in a positive sense. Most people associate work with something unpleasant: the job they hate, the grind, the boredom of the workplace. Negativity has become synonymous with the word work itself.

Though it may be difficult to change one's attitude toward their field of employment, it should not be a challenge in dealing with one's involvement in the world of sports. A generation ago, most people looked at sports as an outlet. Sports were enjoyed and played for the simple pleasures they provided. Sports, in fact, may be the truest kind of work there is. Players cannot take time out in the middle of a game to calculate their play and decide how it will affect their future. They need to play the game to the best of their ability, and let the future take care of itself.

There's no place in sports for excuse makers and sports should never be dealt with in the negative.

We owe it to the present generation, and the ones that will follow, to be motivators.

We owe it in the name of sports, for all the good things that sports has given us. Let's let the corporate jungle motivate for the bottom line. Let's let the Pride of the Yankees, Brian's Song, the Glenn Cunninghams, and the Walter Paytons be the ones to set the example for today's youth. Let's take it upon ourselves to stress the positives and downplay the negatives.

# A CHANCE

Most of the true athletes, the real players, look at their sport and their lives with a sense of gratitude. To be blessed with the physical abilities to perform to the best of your ability is something cherished, and the knowledge that it can all end with the turn of a knee or the crack of a bone makes one truly appreciative. Pushing the envelope of physical endurance has led to amazing accomplishments in the field of sports. Roger Bannister running the four minute mile, a feat thought to be physically impossible, opened the door to a whole new era of distance running. Branch Ricky is having the courage to take a chance on a young player by the name of Jackie Robinson, and together the two would transform the game of baseball into the "Great American Pastime", that would include all Americans. Muhammad Ali's proclamation of being the greatest boxer in the world and having the commitment to take on every challenger, escalating the sport of boxing to a new level, might best describe the impact that confidence can have on a sport. And let us not forget an American hockey team that was made up of college kids, a group of no-names, who gave this nation a great lift by defeating the best team in the world, the Soviets, and bringing home the Olympic gold in the 1980 Olympics.

Sports are made up of great stories, great accomplishments, and great performances that seem to grow with time. They can be found on book shelves and in video stores, and what constitutes their worth is the fact that they were the result of a passion understood only by the true athlete. It's a simple love for a game, a sport, a way of life for which those involved are truly grateful. Those of us who are a little older, and I hope a little wiser, should take it upon ourselves to pass to the next generation the importance and responsibility associated with being included in this special fraternity called athletes.

What is an athlete? The dictionary defines the word as "a person who has the ability or training in sports, games, or other activities requiring physical strength, skill, and endurance". I tend to believe that adjectives, like commitment, heart, desire, and pride, also need to be added to best describe the true athlete. Young people today need to know that athletes are not measured by how much weight they can bench press or how fast they can run the forty-yard dash. They are not judged by earned-run-averages or points-per-game. Their value is not determined by how many autographs they choose to sign, how many endorsements they can pile up, or whether or not they have their own website. The measure of the true athlete is found in the realization of knowing how truly lucky they are, at having been given a chance to do something that they truly love to do and thus they do it well.

More than twenty years ago, I was traveling through a very deep valley in my personal life, when I came to the realization that the only one to blame for my anxiety was me. The following poem was authored at that time and since has become my philosophy of life. I use it to close all of my camp talks and speaking engagements, and I carry a small laminated card in my wallet to help remind me every time I find myself slipping into those regions of negativity. When those feelings start to creep in, I simply pat myself on the backside where that simple card is housed in my wallet and think about the two words that are written on it: "A CHANCE"

# A CHANCE

Today I wake the time has come
My preparations through
I've worked, I've trained, I'm at my best
I know what I can do

One question still bewilders me
I really must ask why
Why am I given all the gifts
When thousands are passed by

Some cannot see, or talk, or hear
Some cannot stand and run
Why am I given all the gifts
Why me the lucky one

What makes me different from the rest
Do I deserve this fate
Why am I given half a chance
of doing something great

The time for talk is over now
It's time that I advance
But in my hearts a special thanks
Because someone gave me a "A CHANCE"

—dah

Throughout our lives, there are certain developments and events that cause us to look at ourselves in a different light. In the late 1980's I was asked if I would be interested in working a summer job run by the United Cerebral Palsy Organization. The job description was that of a camp director, working along with some other teachers and social workers. I was told that we would be working with approximately twenty-five students who were physically and mentally challenged. Seeing that I did not have any other employment for the summer, I decided to accept the position, not knowing exactly what I was getting myself into.

Until that summer, I never had the great fortune of working with special education students, and I must admit that my first day on the job was a little intimidating. I wasn't used to being bombarded with questions as to who I was and where I was from, and I definitely wasn't ready for the handshakes, pats on the back, and even a hug that I received from one of the kids.

In the weeks that followed, we took the kids swimming, played baseball and miniature golf, had a dance, and even went to the movies. We had access to a few vans, so we often loaded them up and took field trips to different playgrounds and other points of interest in our community. The summer passed quickly, and before I realized the six-week summer program had come to an end.

I learned a great deal about myself that summer. I learned that each and every one of us is special, and we should be thankful every day for having been given *A CHANCE* to wake up and *smell the roses.*

I worked that same camp for the next four summers, and I may have done so even longer if the program didn't cease to exist. I remember many of the kids, and I often run into them and their parents. I always make it a point to go over and say hello, and I'm always grateful when they remember me and the good times we shared during those hot summer days.

I've learned a great deal from those kids, and the experience made me a better teacher, coach, and parent. They also taught me that all young people need to realize they've been blessed with some special gifts. They need to know that life gives all of us *A CHANCE,* and it's up to each and every one of us to take that chance and run with it. Sometimes all it takes is to simply look around to see what we have in comparison to others.

With regards to the physically and mentally challenged, I read an article a few years ago about a former professional athlete who was obsessed with the meaning of giving one hundred percent. He referred to the commitment he made, during his playing days, to become the best athlete that he could become and he often questioned his own dedication in the face of injuries and discomfort. He constantly made reference to the boundary lines that athletes strive to surpass and to pushing oneself to go beyond ones capabilities. He believed that all athletes face challenges and must decide whether or not the physical and mental strain is worth it. He thought he knew what giving one hundred percent was all about until he was given the opportunity to spend a few days working with the Special Olympics. How, in just a few days his entire outlook on giving one hundred percent would change.

In the short time period that he spent with these gifted athletes he learned the power of love and human caring. He was amazed at how these exceptional athletes prepared and competed with determination he never anticipated. He talked about giving everything, throwing arms that often did not respond to commands and running on legs that all-to-often did not support them steadily. How they cheered for one another and congratulated one another when their events concluded and the look on their faces as they struggled to the finish lines. He mentioned the feeling that came over him, and how beautiful it was, at the end of the Olympics when these young men and women gathered together to sing the national anthem. And he talked about every athlete receiving a medal and wearing it with pride. He even said he cried as he watched these athletes struggle with an unparalleled determination and he cried when he watched them hug and help each other up when they fell down. He said that it took just two days to finally realize what giving one hundred percent was all about and how his life as an athlete would never be the same.

One doesn't have to work with the Special Olympics or spend a summer working with those who are physically or mentally challenged to appreciate the gifts they possess. I often remind young athletes, in my camp talks, how lucky they are to be blessed with the physical ability to be an athlete. I tell them to take time out and look in the mirror and smile at the person looking back at them. After all, does life really owe us anything more than *A CHANCE?* To be given the chance to play, to learn, to feel, and to compete is something special.

Great athletes, as well as dynamic people in other fields, characteristically respond to the challenges of being the underdog. To defy the odds, to rise to the challenge, to dream the impossible dream, is the way of life to those who attack every day with a passion. Inspirational speakers, coaches, and executives all make reference to the saying, "When the going gets tough; the tough get going". Those who have overcome hardship and loss should be an inspiration to all of us. There are thousands of stories that personify the underdog. We need to read them and we need to apply them to our own struggles. We never know what life has in store for us. That, in itself, should be the ultimate challenge to us all. Facing each day as a new frontier, that unknown entity should be an educational experience that offers us *A CHANCE* to learn something new about ourselves, something that we didn't know when we crawled out of bed that morning.

Our responsibility is to teach it. We need to communicate to the young people in our society that quitting is not an option. We need to make them aware of the value of persistence. This lesson does not just apply to the world of sports but applies to every aspect of their and our own lives. We need to turn around this wrongful attitude, where many young people take stock in the whole world being against them. Today's youth have to realize that life doesn't owe them everything and, if life was kind enough to bless them with some physical and mental gifts, then these gifts have to be nurtured and appreciated. If young people today could begin to realize just how fortunate they really are, then maybe the dropout rates in our schools, the escalating juvenile crime rates, and the "I don't care attitudes" might begin to turn around.

As a high school coach, I would give my players a booklet at the beginning of the season which included motivational stories, as well as expectations associated with education, commitment, and the will to achieve. Having been out of coaching for a number of years, the booklet had been filed away next to some notebooks and playbooks that haven't been opened since my departure from the bench. Quite by accident, while arranging some files, I recently stumbled upon my old handouts. I opened the packet and read the first page, which consisted of a team constitution each of our players was subject to read and sign. The second page was a simple prayer that I had forgotten about but one that defines the importance of *A CHANCE.*

# A Prayer for Today

"This is the beginning of a new day. God has given me this day to use as I will. I can waste it or use it for good. What I do today is important because I am exchanging a day of my life for it. When tomorrow comes this day will be gone forever, leaving in it's place something that I have traded for it. I want it to be gain and not loss, good and not evil, success and not failure, in order that I will not regret the price I have paid for it."

# COACHING

I've spent eighteen years of my life as a high school coach. My coaching resume' would contain a few twenty win seasons, and it would also post some below par years if you based everything on wins and losses. Over the years I learned that each team had an identity and that all players can't be coached the same way.

I remember my first coaching tenure when I was ready to set the coaching world on fire. There would be one way, my way, and that would be it. Everyone had to conform to my philosophy: assistant coaches, players, and managers. All involved with the program would have to toe the line because I had all the answers. The problem I learned, all too soon, was that my way was not a very good way. As the season progressed and our numbers in the loss column were far outgrowing our wins I couldn't understand what was wrong. I started to spread the blame around with clichés like "You can lead a horse to water but you can't make him drink" or "We're small, but we're slow." I was making it a point to convince myself that my players weren't working hard enough and we were short in the talent pool. All in all it made for a miserable year for me and for my players.

There's a profound saying that with age we grow in wisdom; in my case, at least in my coaching education, I believe it to be true. It took me a few years to realize that I had a lot to learn, not only about coaching but also about people. In my later years, I approached the game with a much better attitude. One person who had a great influence on that attitude was my wife. I remember one night, after a very heart wrenching defeat, I returned home and immediately descended the stairs to my wreck room. I sat down, cracked open a cold beer and proceeded to wallow in self-pity. My wife came down to join me and graciously listened to my complaining. When I finished she simply said, "I understand how you feel, but if you think I'm going to go through this after every loss, think again." I came to the realization that she was right. I also came to the realization, about that time in my coaching career, that I was not coaching the game for the same reasons that I played the game—for the simple fun of it. Don't get my wrong, I never enjoyed losing, and I inwardly rejoiced in victory, but I learned that the world still continued to revolve around the sun and rotate on its axis, regardless of whether or not we won a game on a Friday night, and I honestly believe that it made me a much better coach.

Coaching today, at any level, is very difficult. The easy part is the actual time spent with your team in practice and in game situations. The most difficult part is having to deal with all the outside interferences that have a tendency to surround you. I'm talking about being a head coach, not an assistant. I'm not negating the importance of assistant coaches, for they are an essential part of the system. You cannot run a program without loyal help. However, the assistants do not have to shoulder all of the outside responsibilities that the head coach constantly does. I can attest to this in that I served as an assistant coach for two years between head coaching stints. I've often commented to fellow coaches that those two years were two of the most enjoyable of my coaching career. There was nothing like being able to show up for practice, work with some of the players during warm-ups, help out with drills, strategize with the coaching staff at the end of practice, discuss upcoming opponents, and then be able to go home. Being as assistant, I found out, led to a pretty unstressful coaching day. Assistants don't have to worry about bus schedules, practice times, parent problems or any of the other nonsense that has absolutely nothing to do with the game. I recall listening to a respected Division I coach speaking at a coaching clinic, talking about the years he spent as an assistant. He said that he spent ten years as an assistant at three different universities before he got his first head coaching job. He went on to say that, as an assistant, he traveled all over the country and began logging thousands of frequent flier miles while searching for talented players. However, he admitted the longest journey he ever made was the twelve inches up the bench traveling from the assistant coaching seat to the head spot.

The responsibilities that go along with coaching on the high school, college, and professional levels today are tremendous. In the pros, the difficulty of handling athletes making astronomical salaries is mind boggling. The must-win attitude in the Division I college game often forces coaches to recruit players they know full well will only last a year or two before opting for the next level. On the high school level, coaching longevity was once a constant. High school physical education teachers were a stereotype, who more often than not, coached more than one sport.

The game has progressed and specialized so much today that the teacher-coach concept has been long removed. I am not saying that teachers, in today's world, make the best coaches, but it is a realization that when school systems opened up the coaching profession to anyone, they also opened up an avenue for scrutiny. Coach bashing has become an accepted fact. High school coaches, in particular, have been threatened with physical violence. They have become victims of vandalism and intimidation far and away from the court. Coaches' children have been known to be harassed, not just by other children but also by parents of other children. It's no wonder that the longevity of coaching at the high school level has drastically diminished, which has had a decisive negative impact on the high school game and the kids that play it. It is not uncommon for a high school player today to go through his or her four years playing for four different head coaches. Some quality coaches even tend to shy away from school districts that have reputations for coaching turnover.

I remember a meeting I had one night at mid court, prior to a home game, during one of my head coaching stints. The coach who was my opponent that particular night was a veteran coach who was well respected throughout our region, both as a coach and as a teacher. I knew the man fairly well since we coached against each other several times. I'll never forget his opening remarks to me as we approached each other and shook hands. He calmly said, "Are You Crazy? Why would you want to get back into this nonsense?" My answer to this startling question was that there were still a few things that I wanted to try as a coach, and I felt I still had the urge. He told me that this was his last year for sure, because of how the game and everything along with it had changed. He said that coaching was just not the same as when he first started out, and there is not enough time to just deal with basketball. He said that there were far too many people that you have to answer to and try to please. His final comment, prior to the starting buzzer for our game stuck in my head for a long time, knowing that I had nephews, nieces, and my own kids who might one day try out for their high school teams. He said, "Wait until you see the caliber of people who will be coaching high school players ten years from now. Coaches who are in it for all the right reasons will no longer want to do it."

Outside interference, whether from parents, booster clubs, school boards, or fans, should not have a say in a sports program, unless the kids are truly being hurt within the system.

Coaches today need to have some knowledge of the people who are behind the program before they accept a position. I'm not talking about player personnel, but rather an insight into the people who have a say in the program. When I accepted one of my head coaching position I ran into a situation for which I was not prepared, thinking my program would be entirely in my own hands. The job opened during the summer months, and when I was approached about it I was somewhat skeptical. I felt the previous coach did a commendable job, but there were people outside the mainstream who caused him to say, "I had enough". After a few days of indecision I made the call and accepted the position. Over the next few weeks, I proceeded to get my staff together, to meet with some of the returning players, and to start to have some open gyms. Things seemed to be progressing and I began to look forward to the start of the school year and my first season. On Labor Day Weekend, just prior to the start of school, I was preparing to depart for a weekend at the seashore with my family when I received a phone call from my athletic director. He informed me that, at the school board meeting the previous night, the board proceeded to choose my coaching staff for me. I told him that I already had a staff I had been working with, and was under the impression the head coach was allowed to choose his own staff. Don't get me wrong, the staff they chose was made up of some good basketball people, but they were not my people. My immediate response to the athletic director was that my resignation would be turned in on Tuesday, the first day of school. This decision touched off an ugly couple of weeks, and I truly believed that my teaching job was in jeopardy. If it wasn't for one school board member who agreed with my stance and continually tried to convince me to reconsider, I would never have coached at that particular school.

Far too many people, outside of the game, are having an impact on the activities and roles of coaches and players. The coaching profession is losing quality people because of too much outside interference, and the student athlete and the game itself are suffering because of it.

The stress placed on high school coaches today is not just brought on by expectations or projected wins and losses. The stress of dealing with parents, school boards, administrations, and one's own conscience is enough to cut many coaching careers short. I talked to a high school coach who once went through an ordeal with a parent over playing time for his son. The parent invited the coach to take a ride with him, and when the coach got into the front seat of the car his life was threatened. The coach was later compelled to report the incident to school authorities but had to wrestle with his own conscience as to whether or not to push for criminal charges. The coach told me that the man had several children, and he did not want to see the man brought up on charges that could have threatened his livelihood and that of his family, but he was not about to have his own life threatened. He opted not to press charges, and the man later apologized, but the fact remains that coaches today should not be subject to such treatment.

Being out of coaching for a few years now, I am often asked if I miss it and if so what I miss most about it. My answer to this question is always the same. The part of coaching that I miss most is the coaching I did in the spring and fall, what most would consider down time, outside of the season. This was the time when I could lace up my own sneakers and play a little three on three or four on four with some of my players who were not involved in spring or fall sports. It was a time of no pressure, no stress, and no decisions to make. Teams were always chosen by the first three or four players to make a foul shot comprising one team, and the other three or four comprising the other. We often recruited some of my fellow teachers, players of a past generation, to lace them up and mix it up with us. Games were always competitive and intense, where defense always called the fouls, and if there ever was a major discrepancy over a call I would always have the final say. After all, I was the coach! I can honestly say that I do not miss the summer leagues or the team camps. I hated collecting money for the camps, and I hated the paper work and planning that was always associated with it. I do miss the practices and the games, but not nearly as much as the fall and spring open gyms.

These fall and spring workouts were not, by any means, an attempt to persuade players into specialization. They were never mandatory; in fact those involved in fall and spring sports were not allowed to play unless their respective coaches gave them the okay. I, for one, am totally against specialization in high school sports, unless a kid really wants to just play one sport. Far too many kids today are forced into making a decision as to which sport they should play, and usually at far too young of an age. The majority of young athletes today are being led to believe that, for them to excel, they must concentrate on only one sport. I am totally against this philosophy, and this is coming from a guy who only played one sport in high school. Young players should be given the freedom to decide for themselves how they wish to spend their high school careers.

Mark Martino is the athletic director at Lake Braddock High School in Virginia. He's been a teacher for twenty-one years and a coach for nineteen of those. Mark told me that, in a big high school like his, specialization seems to be the name of the game. He believes that the day of the three sport athlete is gone. "Most kids, for fear of not making a team or measuring up to expectations, are throwing everything into one sport." Mark believes, as do other athletic directors that I've talked to, that kids are missing out. High school careers go by so fast and, all-to-often, these young athletes look back and say, "If I had to do it over I would have participated in more than one sport."

High school is and should be a very special four years in the life of a young man or young woman. As a teacher, I see first hand the difficult decisions that young people are faced with each day, and athletics should not be one of them. Specialization in sports should be a decision made by the athlete, but with the support and direction of his or her parents. If a high school athlete wants to specialize or wishes to participate in more than one sport, it is in no way, shape, or form the concern or business of a coach, a mentor, or a community. I can remember, as a high school basketball player myself, being called into the office of the football coach who tried to convince me to play football. When I told the coach that I really loved basketball and that I played it all the time, his answer was that they never practiced on Sundays, and that if I wanted to play basketball it would be okay with him if I played on that day. I couldn't believe what I was hearing, "Okay With Him!

I've heard high school coaches downgrade other sports programs within their school. A propaganda saying that

I've grown to hate is, "Your future could be in this sport." What if a kid really doesn't love that sport? I don't care how much talent a player has, if the love is not strong enough, his or her future in the sport stands little chance. When people give me these lines about what a high school athlete could be if he or she would specialize, I emphatically remind them to consider the kid. I try to impress upon them that the kid has four years of high school, four years that should be among the best years of his or her life. I usually tell them, in no simple terms, "You lived your own high school careers; don't try to live theirs".

Are there coaches today who stress the positives and view the game the way it was meant to be viewed? Of course! Regardless of where the game has been and where the game may be going, there will always be basketball people who will be involved with the game for all the right reasons. I love to watch some of the young coaches wear their enthusiasm and their willingness to learn so brightly. My advice to all of them is to always put the game first and to continually remind their players that it is just a game and not the answer to some question pertaining to their futures.

My hat goes off to the older coaches; the one's who have endured. Many veteran high school coaches, though the numbers seem to be dwindling, still view the game the right way. There's a man presently coaching at my old high school who epitomizes the coaching standards. He recently reached a milestone, winning his four hundredth game. I, like many others, have great respect for this coach, not because of his won-loss record but because of his passion for the game. I also have great respect for him because he is my older brother.

My brother Mick has been a high school teacher for thirty-five plus years and a high school coach for more than thirty of those. He has coached at two different high schools, but his longest tenure has been at his alma mater, where he served four years as an assistant and twenty-six years as the head coach. Mick is a fixture in the coaching ranks of our region. Like most veteran coaches who have progressed through the different generations and changes that incurred, he feels that the game is still a great experience for young men and women. When I asked him what has changed the most over the last twenty years, he smiles and answers, "The pants the players wear are quite a bit longer." "There's a lot more tattoos and pierced body parts today than there were when I first started, but the kids themselves haven't really changed; at least not the ones who really love the game."

Mick's perception of parents is that they are simply that, *parents*. Every parent wants to see their son or daughter achieve great things. Parents, as much as they don't want to admit it, are not coming out on Tuesday and Friday to see the game. They're coming out to see their kid. It doesn't bother them if the team wins or loses, as long as their kid played well. It's not so easy for the coach who views the game differently and has to make decisions on playing time. Mick realizes that it's impossible to keep everyone happy, so you do what you believe, deep down, is best for the team. He believes that most of the time when you have an irate parent, the chances are that when the kid graduates or leaves the program, the parent will never come back to see your team play again, so you're dealing with them for a relatively short period of time. He puts critical fans in the same category: "I don't care if fans are rooting against us or getting on me," "I feel that they've paid their money to attend a game and thereby have the right to yell if they want." He says with a smile, being the avid Yankee fan that he is, that "I often jump out of my chair at home and yell at the T.V. when the manager does something that I don't agree with. It's just the nature of sport and I've leaned not to take it too seriously or too personal." He does agree, however, that coaches and their families should not be subject to antagonizing treatment outside the realm of the game. There are way too many instances of physical attacks on coaches today, and he believes it's one of the reasons so many coaches leave the profession. Many feel it's just not worth it, and it's sad because the game is losing some outstanding teachers.

Mick once told me about a meeting he had with his seniors, prior to the start of a season. He sensed that some of these returnees were not into the game as much as they were as underclassmen, and he wanted to clear the air. He questioned their commitment, and told them that if they were not going to give one hundred percent then he wished, for his sake and for theirs, that they would walk away now. He reminded these young men that he liked each and every one of them, and he didn't want to end the relationship he had with them on a sour note, saying "I don't want to spend years passing each other on the street and not being able to say hello to each other." He reminded them that the game is great, but it's just a game. It's not life, and if they really didn't want it they should do everyone a favor and walk away before it starts. Mick speaks from the heart on occasions like this. He lives in the same town in which he teaches and coaches. He looks forward to stopping at the mini-mart every day for a coffee and running into some of his ex-players. The friendships he has developed over the years with his former players, several of whom are members of his coaching staff, are ones he cherishes deeply.

If there is a concern regarding the game and the changes that he's noticed over the years, it would be the big business attitude that so many people now associate with the game. Million-dollar salaries to kids coming out of high school are restricted to a very small percentage of players. Mick believes that the average high school player should be playing the game for no other reason than to just play. "If they play the game hard and work to become better players, they'll never be sorry." Mick's words are a testament to the truth. All one has to do is check out the high school gym where he coaches on Tuesday and Thursday nights in the off season and you'll find a contingent of his former players, a little older and maybe a little slower, but still showing up to play pickup. Why? As Mick would so simply put it, "Because It's Just A Great Game".

# YOUTH

My first recollection of organized basketball takes me back to the Catholic Youth Organization (CYO) that sponsored a league which included all the Catholic parishes in our town, as well as the surrounding areas. My home was right next door to our church and grade school, and I remember being in third grade when the coach of the team asked me if I'd be interested in being a manager. I thought that it was the greatest job that any kid could ever have. My parents didn't mind, knowing the team practiced in the church hall next door. Not having any baskets in the church hall didn't seem to take away from the practice sessions. I can still recall the older guys working on their passing and dribbling under the direction of Coach Mike O'Brien. Fundamentals were definitely important, something that many youth coaches today deem as non-essential. One of my fondest memories, of those days, was when practice concluded and the team would allow me to tag along, across the back ally, to the local cigar store that also served as a candy store, and to sit in the back room with them over a cold soda.

As I got a little older and I entered the CYO program as a player, we moved up in the world. Two nights a week we were allowed to use the old high school gymnasium for practice and games. We still practiced the same fundamentals—passing, dribbling, and lay-ups, because we were still playing for Coach O'Brien, the same coach who gave me my break as a manager and who devoted a large portion of his life to the youth of our parish. I often think of Mike O'Brien, even today, and in my prayers I thank him for helping to instill in me a love for the game. Seldom do we see coaches of today's youth who coach out of love and respect for the game. More often than not, parents take over youth programs only until their son or daughter graduates, and then they pass it on to the next parent who is waiting in line. It's sad to see the old timers, the ones who ran the same young teams for years, disappear. Like coaches in the higher leagues, many of these dedicated men just don't want to put up with the nonsense or outside interference. Some have actually been asked to step down to make room for this new breed of coaches, or should I say parents.

In addition to our two nights a week in the high school gym, we also traveled on Saturday mornings to the neighboring towns to play some of our rival Catholic schools. Those Saturday morning games were exciting, even though we usually played to a crowd of no more than four people. The reason I remember the number four is because our coach would drive one car and we would always wake my older sister, who was a college student at the time, and talk her into driving the other car. Even though I'm sure it wasn't her idea of how to spend a Saturday morning, she always obliged and actually became a fan.

The other two people who comprised the capacity crowd were, and I can only guess, the older brother or sister of one of the opposing players and their coach. That was it, two teams, two coaches, four fans, and the games were great. Some of the friendships that were born on those early Saturday morning's, between kids from different towns, lasted and matured through high school and beyond. For some reason, I don't ever remember parents sitting in the stands, questioning coach's decisions and yelling instructions to their own kids. No one ever questioned playing time, maybe because everyone played. Come to think of it, I can't even remember if we paid too much attention to whether or not we won or lost. To wear your first uniform, to run warm-up drills before a game, to be part of an organized basketball team...could life for a young kid get any better?

My brother Mick often tells a funny story about his introduction into the game. He recalls being in fifth grade at the same Catholic grade school I attended and playing basketball in the school yard one day with a few of his classmates. One of the nuns, a teacher at the school, walked into the yard and asked my brother and the other boys why they were not practicing with the school team.

The boys informed her that the school team was made up of sixth, seventh, and eighth grade boys and they would have to wait for another year to join. The nun, who was very sports minded and school oriented, went to see the coach one day and asked him about lowering the age requirement to include fifth graders. The coach informed her that there were a large number of boys already on the team, but if the fifth grade boys really wanted to be a part of it then it was all right by him.

My brother remembers being so excited that it didn't even matter to him that there were now forty-four kids on the team. He recalls his first game as a fifth grader and even remembers my mother preparing him some eggs and toast as his pre-game meal. He remembers packing his little gym bag with a uniform that was way too big for him, though it didn't matter because, "he was on the team." He did not get into that initial game, but he confesses that it didn't matter because during warm-ups, with forty-three other kids on the court, he actually got the ball one time and was able to get a shot up. He recalls saying to himself as it left his hands, "What a Game"!

My brother is a great story teller, and he smiles when reminiscing about another game from that first season. The assistant coach on the team wanted to show the boys what a 2-3 zone defense was. Not having a magnetic board, or even a clipboard with a court diagram, he cleared off a table and took out a book of matches that were inside his cigarette pack. He proceeded to break off five matches to use as players in order to design the defense. My brother, being all of ten years old, remember it as being one of the neatest things he ever saw. Imagine, being taught to play a 2-3 zone with matchsticks! He knew he was hooked on the game.

Still one more story from that first season, had to deal with a team from Philadelphia that for some reason made its way up the Northeast Extension and played his CYO team. He claims that he doesn't remember why they played the team, but he does remember an eighth grade kid, on his team, scoring the first basket of the game, and then the Philly squad running off twenty or so unanswered points. By the second half, with the game totally out of reach, Coach Mike O'Brien decided to get everyone into the game. No easy task with forty-four players. My brother remembers an opposing player getting fouled and proceeding to the foul line for two shots. Mike checked a young kid into the game prior to the first shot then substituted for him prior to the second shot. The kid didn't even get the chance to run up and down the floor, but it didn't really matter because he was on the team, and he actually got into a game against players from *The Big City.*

To say that times have changed is a drastic understatement. Basketball, at the lowest level, as with other youth sports, has become a reflection of our society. It is an outcome based stage, controlled by adults who are obsessed with winning and seeing to it that certain kids are put into a position to outshine their peers. Adult involvement, officially and unofficially, has taken the youth game to a level that totally undermines the meaning of youth sports. Today, there are youth athletic boards, bi-laws, and athletic screening. There are coaches checking eligibility requirements, including birth certificates, school districts, parishes, and places of residence. I once witnessed a youth game where the coach wanted to take his team off the floor because the other team had a player whose parents kept him back a year, thus violating a league rule. The coach polled the parents, who were in attendance, hoping that they would agree with his decision to take the team off the court and go home before the game even started. Though some of the parents agreed with him, the majority had enough sense to tell the coach that they didn't come to a game to take their kids home. I was overjoyed to hear some of them say, "Play the game." The thing that amazed me most about this particular incident was that no one asked the players whether or not they wanted to go home or whether or not they cared about this one particular player. I'm willing to wager what their answer would be.

I've learned that one of the most highly contested issues today that infuriates youth coaches, is the decision made by some parents to keep their kids back a year. Different states have different rulings, I'm sure, but in our state a student athlete can compete at the age of nineteen as long as he or she does not turn nineteen before the start of the respective season of participation. A student athlete, according to our state rules, can also compete on the interscholastic level for a total of six seasons, grades seven through twelve. Parents sometimes look into private schools for a year and are willing to pay the tuition to allow their child this extra year to develop. Since most public schools frown on this practice, particularly if a student is successfully passing a grade, the contention arises as to whether the student, being in private school and not subject to interscholastic rules, should be allowed to participate in extra curricular activities for that private school. I'm primarily talking about the junior high level, since most private high schools in our state belong to the state interscholastic organization and compete within the same leagues as the public schools. Players are also allowed only four years of varsity participation.

Many youth coaches, who do not have one of these "red shirt" players, rant and rave against this practice. In our area, for example, the Catholic Youth Organization will not allow a student who enters one of their schools as an eighth grader to participate in any CYO sports if that students is staying back that year. Personally, I think the rule is ridiculous. I see nothing wrong with keeping a son or daughter back a year if it is in the best interest of the child, as long as the child is within the age limitation. Some children mature late, both physically and mentally, and the extra year can add to their confidence and self-esteem. What's the difference in starting a child a year late entering first grade or holding them back in seventh or eighth? Youth coaches tell you, "Winning isn't everything." Those who protest the legal retention of a student are only concerned with how much of an impact that student will have on their chances to win a title.

Coaches must be made aware that their sole obligation is to the kids involved in their program, and I'm talking about ALL the kids. I recently talked to a youth league coach who informed me that, in their youth league, the starters are required to play the first quarter of a game and then they must sit the entire second quarter. He proceeded to tell me about a coach who made it a point to save one of his more talented players so that he could insert him into the game every second quarter. The kid would invariably dominate the quarter, and it was not uncommon for some players, on his own team, to never even get to touch the ball. He told me when he approached the coach and questioned this action, the coach justified his position by saying that the kid did not play in the first quarter, so legally he could play in the second. Trying to explain that this was not the intention of the rule, the questioning coach was snubbed and told, "Then they should change the rule."

Can youth coaches be so naive as to actually believe that winning games or even championships at this level somehow sets them apart from other coaches? Do they not realize, at this level, that the kids who are physically stronger and have matured early will usually win despite their tutelage? Many of these coaches also have become the great "I—We" men of the coaching ranks. When asked whether the team won or lost a game, their usual reply is "I Won, or We Lost" and those two words are never reversed. Do they not realize that the score of a game is of little consequence when dealing with the lives of the young people who have been put in their trust?

A few years back I read a column in the Reading Eagle Newspaper, written by Mike McGovern, who, at the time was the assistant sports editor and columnist. McGovern is one of my favorite sports writers. I always look forward to reading his column, due to his understanding of today's sports issues. The article was titled, "Parents Are Still Taking the Joy Out Of Kids Games." McGovern stated that in 1981, The National Youth Coaches Association (NYSCA) was founded for the purpose of training volunteer coaches. The training was set up to help set team rules, understand why kids quit sports, and what kids expect from sports. It was also designed to help structure drills and practices, so that the main objectives were learning and having fun. The next paragraph contained a statistic that ultimately floored me. McGovern stated, "And less you think that kids don't have fun while playing their games, statistics show that 70% of kids drop out of sports by the time they're 13 years of age." Thirteen years of age! I couldn't believe what I was reading. My first thoughts were that kids today are quitting sports before they're even old enough to fall in love with them. "The number one reason why!" "They're not having fun."

McGovern's column went on to say that nearly twenty years ago, before youth sports became an obsession, a lot of folks regarded the NYSCA as unnecessary. People scoffed at the idea that volunteer coaches should have to go through any kind of training, said Fred Engh, president of the National Alliance for Youth Sports (NAYS), an organization set up for kids, parents, and coaches.

McGovern says, "These days, coaches can use all the help they can get. For proof, all you have to do is keep up with the news." He went on to give a few examples, one involving more than 100 adults ("goodness knows, the term is used loosely"), who ended up in a slugging match on the field after a football game involving 11 and 12 year-olds. The incident, it is believed, was started when an assistant coach began taunting players, coaches, and parents from the opposing team. The article goes on to say that while the adults were taking things into their own hands-and-fists, the players watched from the stands and the field. Another incident had to deal with a man and his brother beating a high school coach for the man's son's lack of playing time. Both men were sentenced to forty-five days in jail.

These types of incidents are not confined to certain areas within our country. They are not based on socio-economic or cultural regions. They are happening in grade school gymnasiums, on youth playing fields, and in pee wee hockey rinks. McGovern goes on to say, "I wonder if any of these parents, who are so quick to mix it up and go overboard when it comes to sports, are similarly concerned with the progress their kids make in Math, or Science, or English, or History. You know things that really matter."

The article concludes by saying that the sad thing is that for all the attention these incidents receive in the media, and for all the upheaval they cause in their communities, the parents involved are still blind to the reality that they are the problem. He goes on to say that some leagues and athletic associations, in order to make those offending parents see the light of day, have gone so far as to require all parents to undergo sportsmanship training, administered by Parents Association of Youth Sports (PAYS). Should parents refuse, then their kids cannot participate.

Part of the training includes adhering to a Code of Ethics. Two of the promises in the Code are worth mentioning and memorizing:

1. I will remember that the game is for youth and not adults.
2. I will do my very best to make youth sports fun for my child.

McGovern's final line seems to sum up the problem perfectly, "You'd think those things, basic as they are, would be givens. Unfortunately, they're not."

Parents of a past generation, at least the majority of them, viewed sports in a much different light. It's not that parents didn't care about their kids, for nothing can be farther from the truth. Parents merely looked at sports in a different manner: happy that their kids were participating and glad that their kids were enjoying themselves. Parent back then didn't attend every game, and you would never see them at a practice. A good friend of mine remembers playing Little League Baseball. His mother confessed to him years later that she absolutely loved it when he and his brother left for the baseball field, knowing that for the next two hours she would have some peace and quiet around the house and how she looked forward to that small respite of solitude. This past fall, I happened to be driving by a field one evening and witnessed a large contingent of people sitting on lawn chairs watching some kind of game. I was compelled to stop and see what was going on. When I parked my car and walked toward the field, hoping to see a rivalry game of some sort in progress, I was taken back when I realized it was nothing more than a pee wee football practice.

When I hear about parental involvement in their child's sport, I often think of a story that had to do with probably the best high school player ever to come out of my high school. The player in question was six foot six and in the 1960's led his team to the Eastern Finals of the state tournament. He was chosen first team All-State and was recruited by a number of large universities. The boy's mother died when he was young, and his father owned a barroom. The boy's father never saw him play a high school game until one night a friend of the family talked him into going along with him. The two men sat in the top row of the bleachers and were surrounded by a full house of cheering fans. The boy had a monster game that evening, and as the final outcome of the game was becoming fundamental the coach substituted for the boy, who was given a rousing standing ovation which seemed to last forever. When the team entered the locker room, one of his teammates asked him if he knew his father was in the stands. The boy, feeling pretty good, walked into his father's bar later that night and a few of the regulars congratulated him, but his father never said a word. Later that night, after cleaning up, the boy said to his father, "I heard you were at the game tonight." His father replied, "Oh yeah, you played well. By the way, don't forget tomorrow when you wake up you have to clean up around the bar."

As I said, it's not that parents didn't care a generation ago. It's just that they tended to put the game in its proper place. I truly believe that more kids played back then because they were not under the scrutiny of their parents, and were not being told that they had to excel. Most kids played because it was just a game.

Another great high school player from the 1960's recently told me that he definitely would not play sports if he were a kid today. How can it possibly be fun for kids who are constantly being critiqued by adults? I'm surprised kids today even go out for teams knowing that their play will be scrutinized.

Parents and coaches are not the only adults to blame. Organizations and services have actually profited at the expense of youth sports. In the November 25, 2002 issue of Sports Illustrated, Rick Reilly wrote an article entitled— *Dribblephilia*. The story was about a five foot one inch, ninety pound, fifth grade kid who was ranked as the top <u>fifth grade</u> basketball player in the nation. Reilly's article pinpointed *Hoop Scoops* Online.com, one of the best known websites for coverage of Blue Chip recruits, as the service that did the ranking. The article states that the reason kids are ranked at this level is that college coaches want to know, so kids' names are put out there, and if they turn out good, then you were the first to write about them.

In defense of their position the ranking service says that college coaches, knowing that they have to beat Kentucky, Duke, and North Carolina have to get the star players onto their campus when they're in junior high." Junior high school! Give me a break! The article goes on to say that it isn't only college coaches. High school coaches, AAU coaches, even shoe companies want to know. Reilly uses the example of Leon Smith and Korleone Young. Both ranked number 1 in their class as middle school players and turned pro right out of high school, both out of the NBA today.

Another article dealing with this problem showed up in the *Washington Post* on February 24, 2003. The column was written by Preston Williams and was titled: *A New*

*Meaning for Playground Basketball*—Ranking Systems Put Spotlight on Youngsters. Williams refers to the same young kid, now a sixth grader, as having an "eye-popping resume ; national title, all-star game appearances, prestigious camp invitations and hobnobbing opportunities with Shaquille O'Neal, Yao Ming and even Adam Sandler." Like Reilly, Williams pinpoints online recruiting publications *Hoop Scoop* as the source behind the ranking. Quotes from psychologists, coaches, and recruiting analysts are featured and all agree that ranking players at early ages can be harmful, no matter how impressive their stats might be. Williams quotes Tom Konshalski, a well know recruiting analyst, after he was introduced to the "fourth best fourth grader in New York". "I think it is a subtle form of child abuse: rating young players doesn't help anyone."

The article quotes Jay Bilas, who is an ESPN sports analyst and former Duke player, as saying, "How are you going to tell anything from a fifth-grader? You might be able to say a kid has some ability relative to his age group, but I just don't see anything good that can come out of that. It would be like a company going out and starting to recruit kids when they're in fifth grade. Could you imagine Xerox or any big company recruiting fifth-graders? We've got our eye on you, son."

William's article also quotes Maryland coach Gary Williams and Michigan State coach Tom Izzo. Williams believes ranking kids really doesn't mean anything. "Most coaches recruit players who can help their program the way they like to play." Izzo admits that he has looked at information on young kids but says "the recruiting process hurts more kids than it helps. I think we're part of the problem instead of part of the solution".

Can we really predict how a young player will mature? I personally know a few active college coaches, and I asked each of them how interested they were in the ability of junior high school players. Each and every one of them answered the same way, "Don't be ridiculous."

I, too, agree with the assessment on Tom Konchalski. Ranking kids at the grade school level should be labeled child abuse. The pressures that could follow a kid with a label like the best in his or her age group may become too much to handle. What happens if they fall short of their expectations? What if they just stop loving the game? Those who rank these kids have to look at the whole picture. They're dealing with young kids here, not commodities. Those doing the ranking, as well as coaches who are involved, should be made accountable.

The exploitation of athletes is nothing new to the world of sports. However, the hype and attention given to athletes in today's world has been filtering down to such a young age that it has taken away from the game itself. Young players feel that they have to outdo the other players on their teams. They're often pitted against each other, and the team and the outcome of the game are of little consequence. The sensationalizing of young players today has become a standard; and the respect for the beauty of the game has become a thing of the past.

ESPN's December 15, 2002 "Between the Lines" with Bob Ley, focused on the topic Exploitation of Young Athletes. Billy Packer, Dick Vitale, and Sonny Vaccaro were on the panel to discuss the delicate issue. The program aired just three days after the December 12th match-up of LeBron James' St. Vincent-St.Mary's team against national power Oak Hill Academy. The game was broadcasted in prime time on ESPN2.

Billy Packer blamed the media for sensationalizing young athletes to the extent of infecting the game. He stated that the fact that the U.S. men's team finished 6th in the World Games that year attests to the demise of the game in our country. He attacked the hype given to LeBron James, and even went so far as to name players he felt were better high school players, at their time, than James is now. Arguments followed from Vitale, who defended his position of singing the praises of LeBron, to Vaccaro, who defended his position on the value of AAU exposure. However it was Packer's attack on the system and the state of American basketball that took center stage.

Do we need sports experts to convince us that a problem exists? Does it take a sports psychologist to open our eyes to the fact that the hype and exploitation of players is causing a problem? Can we, the average fan, average parent, and average coach, asses the problems

DAVID HOLLAND

with the game on our level? For the sake of the game, I hope and pray that we can try.

Sportsmanship training for parents and coaches is a step in the right direction towards curbing some of the problems associated with youth sports today. Children love their parents and respect their coaches and whether we realize it or not, we are the models for our kids and our players. We need to put ourselves in their shoes. We need to remember what it was like to be ten or eleven years old. Kids want to please their parents. They long for the compliments bestowed upon them by parents and coaches for performing well. Look into your child's eyes when you say, "great game" and compare it to the look in their eyes when you chastise them for playing poorly. If your words are bringing your son or daughter to tears, then something is drastically wrong. If coaches are berating young kids to the point of turning them off to the sport, then something is drastically wrong. If kids aren't having "FUN" playing sports at a young age, than something is drastically wrong.

As parents and coaches we need to take a step back. We need to realize that it's really not that important, that it's just a game. More important still is the fact that it's their game, not ours. If we do not learn to lighten up on our kids, we may not only turn them away from sports, we may also turn them away from more important things that can have a lasting impact on their lives. The fear of failing, of not measuring up to expectations, has caused both physical and mental problems among our youth. Stories about kids developing ulcers at an early age are common today, as well as stories of kids withdrawing from schoolwork and participation for fear of being singled out. Has it become easier to just give up rather than having to deal with the realization of letting someone down? The sad reality to this scenario is that the person they feel they are letting down is, more often than not, the person they really need most in their lives.

The lasting effects we may unknowingly be subjecting our kids to may even be life threatening. The Center For Disease Control and Prevention recently released documentation on the alarming rise in obesity in our society. It seems the number of Americans that are extremely obese (at least 100 pounds overweight) has quadrupled in recent years, and the statistics are filtering down to our youth. In the September 22, 2003 issue of *Sports Illustrated*, Rick Reilly's column entitled, "*The Fat of the Land*" attests to the fact that, over the last twenty years, the number of overweight children in our country has doubled. According to the Center For Disease Control, one of three kids born in 2000 will contact type 2, diabetes—and potentially heart disease, blindness, asthma, sleep apnea, gall bladder disease and depression that may come with it—because they are obese.

Are we, as adults, as much to blame for the amount of calories that our kids devour throughout the course of a day? Are we contributing to the dropout rate in kids' sports by adding to the idol time and unhealthy lifestyles of our youth? Pediatricians look at the problem of youth obesity as an epidemic. We need to take a long, hard look at youth sports, for the positives, and we need to get our kids moving in the right direction.

Recently I attended a workshop for youth coaches. The opening speaker was a physiologist who delivered a presentation on the physical capabilities of young athletes. Issues, ranging from the amount of recovery time needed by young athletes in comparison to high school and college athletes, to the treatment of injuries for the different maturity levels, were brought up. The presenter hammered on the fact that so many young athletes today arc being injured by overworking their joints and muscles without proper recovery time. He said that weekend tournaments that can exceed five or six games can be devastating to young kids. Injuries from overuse, especially in sports like basketball and soccer where excessive running is the norm, have produced more injuries than ever before. He said that burnout is not just mental but also physical, and young players can physically be damaged to the point of ending careers before they ever start. He used the example of kids throwing curve balls at a young age and how the stress on the arm has ended their pitching careers long before they ever reached adolescence. He told the crowd that a lot of big league pitchers today were actually outfielders who strengthened their arms by naturally throwing hard. He finished by reminding coaches of the type of athletes they are coaching. He reminded them that the well being of these young athletes is in their hands and that well being can easily be damaged.

The next speaker was a veteran high school coach who talked about motivation and the treatment of players. He touched on the importance of having a respectful relationship between players and coaches, and humorously hinted that the game, and how it's perceived, has changed since the time he first started coaching.

The final speaker of the day dealt with regulations and legal ramifications that can have serious liability implications on coaches and sponsoring schools. I couldn't help but wonder if youth coaches a generation ago had to listen to these concerns.

I left the seminar a little more knowledgeable about the applicable laws and the do's and don'ts associated with the coaching of young athletes, and I couldn't help but feel that a much bigger issue was ignored. No one, throughout the entire seminar, spoke about the obligation that the coaches in attendance have to the young players on their teams. No one mentioned the importance that coaches place on winning and to what limits they would go to secure victory. No one asked about playing time and how they plan on handling it. These are the issues that need to be addressed and that every youth coach needs to deal with.

Someone needs to make it known that trophies and banners are not the job description. The sole purpose is to get kids interested and to give every kid an opportunity to fall in love with the game, so they will continue to want to play it. There's no doubt in my mind that the reason these topics weren't brought up was out of fear of retaliation and because of the looks of disgust from the members in attendance. I can often tell who the complainers are by their youth league championship jackets or coaching shirts that they wear so proudly. The concept of bringing youth coaches together is admirable, but the message that they need to hear is downright crucial.

I realize I am not being fair to all those youth coaches who are into it for all the right reasons. Those of you and you know who you are, have my gratitude and respect. You are the one's making a positive difference in the lives of our youth.

I recently had the pleasure of sitting down with a youth coach who's been coaching the same team for over thirty years. The man's dedication and commitment to kids and the game itself should somehow be rewarded. Norm Brown of Minersville, Pennsylvania has been the coach of St. Vincent's boys CYO basketball team for more than three decades. He credits his longevity to the simple enjoyment of working with kids and also in having the opportunity to coach at a supportive school. Norm's one of those guys who remembers every past player and the years they played for him. He smiles as he talks about so many of the young men who came through his program, and he takes pride in the fact that many of them continued playing at the high school level. When I asked Norm about changes affecting the game today, he said kids today are forced to make decisions regarding the game at much too early an age. "Too many young kids feel they have to look ahead instead of just playing for the love of it. I've never tried to sway a kid to attend a particular high school; I've always felt that should be a decision set aside for the player and his parents."

Norm's biggest fear is that the number of kids participating today, in comparison to the past, is falling. Schools are actually having a hard time getting enough kids to field a team, and the leagues are losing schools. Some CYO programs have actually consolidated with other schools, and this has caused some problems with overloading talent, thus further diminishing the numbers due to kids quitting. Many kids today aren't giving themselves a chance to see if they really like the game, and many adults aren't helping the situation by placing too much emphasis on winning.

There's a book titled, "Just Let the Kids Play", written by Bob Bigelow with the help of Tom Moroney and Linda Hall. I strongly recommend it to every parent and to every youth coach. In fact, I believe that the book should be mandatory reading for all concerned. Bigalow does not just focus on the sport of basketball, though he was a former college and professional player, but on all organized youth sports.

His in-depth study of the problems facing the youth games of today is an eye opening experience for the reader. Bigelow looks at elite teams, parental involvement, specialization, and coaching for all the wrong reasons, as some of the major concerns. He documents why kids are burning out, suffering from overuse injuries and mental stress, which is leading so many kids to quitting at younger and younger ages. More importantly, the book offers some solutions to the problems. I strongly urge every parent, coach, and fan who has a stake in the matter to do yourself and your children a favor and read this book.

Is there anything in this world more important to us than our children? Is there a parent among us who doesn't want to see his or her daughter or son do well? Aren't we, as parents, willing to do anything within our power to secure our children's success or have we gone to extremes to guarantee that our kids will outshine other kids, regardless of the costs? We need to take a long look at these questions, and more importantly, we need to be truthful about our answers. We need to know the adults who are having an impact on our children's lives. We need to know their teachers, their coaches, and the parents of their friends. We need to take a good look at ourselves, and we need to determine whether or not we're doing the best for our kids. We need to realize that the best for them may not constitute paving the way for them. Most importantly, we need to think like a kid thinks and to remember what it was like to be their age. We need to learn to accept our kids and look out for them because they are our kids, not because of some far off utopian life that we envision for them.

A few years ago I remember being hit with a snowstorm that shut down the school districts in our area for three days. A snow day to school children is like Christmas. Kids have a smile on their face that seems to get bigger with each inch of snow that accumulates. My daughter Kelsey, who was nine-years-old and in fourth grade at the time, spent each day playing outside with the kids in the neighborhood. On the evening of the second day off, when she returned home for supper, after giving my wife and me a play by play of the day's events, asked me if I wanted to go out later and do some sleigh riding with her. Upon completion of a hearty meal, we bundled up and proceeded to pull our sled up the hill of our backyard. For the next hour, the world was ours. We tumbled down the mountain blazing new trails with each run. We got our faces covered with snow, and we laughed when we fell off our sled before reaching the bottom. We took turns riding in front and back, and we even threw a few snow balls at each other. As we lay in the snow making perfect angels, it occurred to me that there's going to come a time when Kelsey's not going to want to ride on the sled with her Dad anymore. Next year she's going to be ten, and before I know it those teenage years will arrive, and Dad and snowstorms will be put on the back burner. I took a long look at her red cheeks and her runny nose, and I realized, for the first time in I don't know how long, how wonderful winter can be. Although the two of us were reaching the freezing point, and knowing some milk and cookies awaited us before we would retire to our beds, I couldn't help but ask Kelsey if she'd do me one favor. She said, "Sure Dad, what do you want? I said, "Just One More Ride Down That Hill".

# FRIENDSHIPS

# FRIENDSHIPS

As mid-life gets its grip on us
and we show some wear and tear
we must look back on our yesterdays
when we didn't have a care.

When we grew up in the playgrounds,
on the ball-fields, and the streets
and the store down at the corner
where, as kids, we'd always meet.

We played a lot of pickup games,
the school yard was like home.
We wore out many pairs of Chucks
and we never were alone.

We waited for the block parties,
the dances, and the games.
We came from different parts of town,
neighborhoods that had great names.

Our town was our entire world
from east end to the west.
There were not enough hours in the day,
our youth was just the best.

How did it pass so quickly?
We grew up much too fast.
But memories will always hold
the great times of our past.

We move in different circles now,
our jobs take up our time.
We follow things our own kids do,
seeing that they toe the line.

And in doing so I only hope
as their years race by so fast.
They may look back on their youth and know
Great Friendships Always Last!

—dah

If you want to invest some money in the basketball development of your son or daughter, I strongly recommend sending them to an overnight camp on a college campus run by a college coach and his or her staff. I truly believe, especially for the middle school age kid, that college camps are not only a great learning experience in terms of basketball, but can also be a tremendous learning experience in terms of life. Note that I am not talking about exposure camps, which are set up solely to showcase players. I like the college camps because the coach usually fills his or her staff with college players and local high school coaches. The head coach always conducts an initial meeting reminding his or her staff that this is a camp, a business that succeeds or fails by how enjoyable the experience is for each and every camper. Most coaches preach the main goal as being a positive experience for each kid, so they will want to come back again next year.

College camps teach fundamentals, something many youth programs have forgotten. The kids also play a lot of games in the course of the week. The best thing about camp games is the fact that there is no pressure placed on winning and losing. There is also no pressure on individual performance since parents, fans, and spectators are at the bare minimum. By playing a lot of games, players seldom have time to celebrate a victory or wallow in defeat since they may be scheduled to play again, on the next court over, just a few minutes after the completion of their game. At a college camp that I had the pleasure of working last summer, I remember refereeing a great game in the thirteen and fourteen age group. The contest came down to the final shot in which a little guard let go a jumper that hit nothing but net as the final buzzer went off. Everyone rushed the court to congratulate the kid, but within five minutes the team was scheduled to play another game, and the heroics and excitement was forgotten as soon as the ball was tossed up.

Most of the coaches whose camps I've worked over the years, stress the number system when dealing with playing time in camp games. At the start of the week each player on a team is given a number. The method of assigning numbers does not matter. Some coaches allow the players to pick their numbers out of a hat. Some try to assign numbers to try to balance tall players and short players. The method really doesn't matter because all of the players, throughout the course of the week, will play with different players at different times. The way the number system works is as follows; suppose there are eight players on a team, the initial game will start with the players whose numbers are one through five. At four minutes into the game, numbers six, seven, and eight will replace one, two, and three. At the next four minute interval, number one, two, and three will replace four, five, and six and so on throughout the game. At the start of the next game, numbers two through six will start, and at four minutes seven, eight, and one will replace two, three, and four. This practice of substitution will continue throughout the week. By the end of the week, every kid on the team will start a game, finish a game, and play with every player on the team.

The number system is not exclusively reserved for camps. I believe that youth programs would especially thrive due to its benefits. The team concept that is created by every player's involvement gets everyone interested. Coaching actually becomes easier by not having to worry about playing time. Young kids become better all around players because they are not plugged into a certain position. If the "true point guard" is out of the game then someone else has to take over the spot, and if the big men are on the bench then players have to find a way to adapt. After all, isn't that what happens all too often when they do get to high school? The number system also creates greater team unity. If a player knows it's his or her time to sit then there will be no long faces or dejections. Kids on the bench are behind their teammates and know that their teammates will support them back, when the four minutes are up and they re-enter the game.

One summer, I had the great pleasure of coaching a youth team made up of twelve and thirteen year-old boys. We played in a summer league which was comprised of a number of junior high school teams from the surrounding area. We had eight players on our team, and we used the number system from start to finish. In our final game, we were ahead by a few points late in the second half with one of our stronger players sitting on the bench. I looked at this kid as he sat next to me, and I thought it was great how he was not sulking for not being in the game at this crucial time. He was totally into the game, and he was cheering his teammates on with great enthusiasm. He understood it was not his ability but rather the rotation of the number system that had him sitting, and he accepted it and, I believe, benefited from it. We ended up losing that game by a few points and I remember a parent, not one of my player's parents but rather a parent from the opposing team, who came up to me and asked, Why did you sit that kid at the end of the game? You might have won the game if he was in there. My answer was, "Yes, maybe we could have but at what price?" I told him that these kids developed friendships over the summer. They respected each other and worked as a team—a team consisting of all eight players equally. I went on to explain that my only goal in coaching this team was to make each of the players a little better and to instill in them the love for a great game. When I walked out of the gym that night many of the players thanked me for coaching them and told me they had fun. The number system is a wonderful way of keeping kids mentally and physically involved in the game. I know it's just wishful thinking, but wouldn't it be great to see all youth programs adopt it.

Getting back to the college basketball camps, aside from basketball, these camps offer kids a good look at college life. Campers stay in dormitory rooms where they live with a roommate, they eat cafeteria food provided by the college, and they make friends with kids from different areas. It always amazes me, on the last day of camp, how many kids are exchanging phone numbers and e-mail addresses and making plans to see each other again next year.

College coaches are adamant when challenging campers to meet new kids throughout the week long camp. I think it's great to see new friendships develop all in the name of the game. I remember a few years back, when our family was taking a summer vacation, having a layover in the Pittsburgh airport. (Pittsburgh is at the other end of the state from where we live.) My son D.J., who at the time was eleven years-old, was walking through the airport with me when a young boy yelled out his name and waved to him. Surprised, I said to my son, who was that kid? He answered that he was a kid that was at camp with him earlier in the summer.

Another great camp story that comes to mind involved my nephew, Mike Rhoades. When Mike was in sixth grade I had the opportunity to take him to a college camp in Willow Grove, Pa. The boys lived in cabins and played on outdoor courts, and the combination of city kids and rural kids tended to give the style of the game an interesting twist. It was Mike's first camp and he simply loved it, but it wasn't until years later that the camp took on a special meaning for him. In 1994, when his college team was playing in the Division III national semi-final game in Buffalo N.Y., he couldn't help but notice during warm-ups that a kid from the opposing team looked familiar. This opposing player must have felt the same connection, for he too stared at Mike across the mid-court stripe. After the game was over and they shook hands, the two questioned each other as to where they had met. They came to the realization that it was back in sixth grade at the camp in Willow Grove, Pa. many years before, where they actually played on the same team.

College camps can be a great avenue for the discovery of new friendships. Being away from home, maybe for the first time in your child's life, can be a memorable experience, and the college camp with caring coaches and kids from different areas can make the experience a great one. I highly recommend, at some point in your young player's life, investing some money to send him or her to a college basketball camp.

I can go on and on about the valuable friendships solidified through this wonderful game. When I speak at camps and clinics, I never bypass the chance to tell young players that the greatest gift the game of basketball has ever given me is the best friends in my life. I try to remind them that wins and losses are not as important as they might think. Points per game, rebounds, and assists, will soon be forgotten, but friendships can last for a lifetime. When I think back to my high school days, I honestly cannot remember our record, or final scores, or even great moments on the court, but I can remember my teammates—the guys with whom I played throughout my high school career. I also tell young players that it's been thirty years since I graduated from college and I still keep in touch with many of my college teammates. Some of us still get together every summer to share a long weekend, drink a few beers, and reminisce about our college days.

What's even greater is the fact that our kids have become friends with each other. I'm talking about guys from Pennsylvania, New Jersey, Massachusetts, and New Hampshire, all with kids and busy schedules, making time for each other after thirty years. Sometimes it amazes me how a simple game can have such a lasting impact on the lives and relationships of those who shared it.

When I consider the friendships and the great people I've met through the game, I can't help but feel grateful. If anyone would have told me, back when I was that manager for the CYO team, the game would reward me with such great friends, I probably would not have believed them. How could I possibly have known, growing up in a small town, that a simple game, played with a bouncing ball, would have such an impact on my adult life?

The game of basketball, as with other sports, can offer so much to the young people of today, if they would just play it for the game that it is. It really doesn't matter if you are a starter on your high school team or not. Whether you play at the college level or spend your free time in college playing intramurals. Whether you're playing on your grade school youth team, or taping yourself together at the age of fifty to play pickup games on Thursday nights (with the same guys you've been competing against for the past twenty years), the game of basketball is still a game. The friendships are irreplaceable, the workout is by far the best, and the gratification can only be understood by those who play.

The game of basketball also helps us break down the ridiculous social barriers society has established over the years. Friendships, developed through the game, are not based on religious affiliations, race, or socio-economic patterns. The kid leading the fast break doesn't stop to ask the kid filling the lane how much money his or her parent makes or what church he or she attends. And the only color that matters to the eyes of a young point guard is that the jersey of the kid who is about to receive the bounce pass to finish off the fast break is the same color jersey as he or she is wearing.

Movies like *Remember the Titans* can show the power athletics can have over cultural barriers. The respect that can be earned through a simple game is one that can withstand the pressures sometimes brought on by society. Competitiveness often brings out the best in humans. What basketball fan can forget the classic match-ups of Magic Johnson and Larry Bird? From their college days through their outstanding professional careers, these two men, of different backgrounds and different races, generated a respect for each other and for their profession due to their undying passion—Their Love for the Game!

So many books have been written and so many movies have been made about the heartwarming friendships cultivated through sports. There's a certain respect athletes develop, not through trash talk or boastfulness, but through honest competition that only those involved can understand. To watch two opposing high school kids play their hearts out for thirty-two minutes and then embrace at the end of the game is what it's all about. To hear a kid compliment his teammates and his opponent is a lesson we all need to embrace. My dad often said the world would be a much better place to live if all of the world's leaders were athletes. He truly believed that the social, ethnic, and political differences that produce lasting enemies might be alleviated with the simple toss of a ball.

Friendships that were born and nurtured through the game can last a lifetime and often do. It must have something to do with a type of respect, rightfully earned through competition, which creates such a bond. My best friend growing up was a kid by the name of Billy Roberts. "Harpo" was his nickname due to his blond curly hair and the fact that nearly everyone in my hometown had a nickname. We met when we were both Little Leaguers but our friendship grew and solidified when we both fell in love with the game of basketball. Harpo and I would spend hours in the playground. We played on the same high school team and, even though he was two years ahead of me and I was fortunate enough to start ahead of him, it didn't affect our friendship at all. I will always remember, when wc were just young kids, we would play two-on-two games to one hundred points against two kids from the opposite end of town. The series would be seven games and we would play two at our playground, two at theirs, and if their was a seventh game needed, which for some reason there always seemed to be, we would flip a coin to see which court would be the host. I can't recall how many series we played against those kids, but I can still remember the walks home from their playground when Harpo and I would relive the games. Billy and I are still great friends today though we don't see much of each other. A few years back I was asked to speak on his behalf when he was honored as the Man of the Year for his commitment to a social organization back in our home town. I felt I could have talked all night about the great times we had growing up.

Someone once said, "In order to get by in this world you need to have three good friends." I have always taken this statement very seriously. Real friendship is priceless, and it is forged over many years. In this fast paced world that tends to dominate our lives, we seldom take the time to call an old friend or to make plans to meet for a cup of coffee. We get caught up, unknowingly, viewing others as commodities with a "what can you do for me attitude", and tend to forget the importance of sustaining real friendships. Maybe it takes just a simple thing like the love of a game to produce friendships. In my frequent talks to the youth of our game I always make a point of raising my five fingers up into the air and I tell the kids in the audience that, in all the years I've been around the game, I have never met five people associated with the game that I can honestly say I hated. However, I then go on to tell them that if they all put both of their hands in the air and multiplied the number of fingers on both hands by ten, they would still fall short of the number of great people I've met through the game.

There's something to be said about the game being "bigger than the people who play it". In many ways the game has helped mold me, and so many of my hoop-head buddies, into the adults that we've become. It instilled in us a sense of knowledge, a sense of what's right and wrong, and a sense of commitment and determination to face everyday challenges, and it has surrounded us with friends who live by the same credence.

# HEROES

# HEART

I'm not a gifted scholar
In that I'm rather weak
In wealth, in rank, in stature
My outlook may be bleak

I'm not a well known figure
No Lincoln, Brahms, or Ruth
My strength lies in my presence
In faith, in love, in truth,

I'm thankful for the good things
That money cannot buy
I have my legs, my arms, my eyes
How fortunate am I

So do not judge me harshly
For I'll finish what I start
And judge me not by size or strength
Please judge me by my heart!

—dah

When we were kids, the older guys were everything. To see a high school player walking down the street wearing his letterman jacket or sweater was like viewing royalty. We dreamed of one day having one of those jackets with our names on the front and our school insignia and participating sport proudly displayed on the back. To have a high school athlete give us the time of day, or maybe take some time to shoot some baskets with us before the playground games began, was like winning the lottery. I guess we considered them our heroes, because they were exactly what we wanted to be.

It was strange that after they graduated there was always another hero to take their place. We watched the pros and the college guys on T.V., and we idolized many of them, but they were out of reach. Most young players of my generation never looked too far ahead in terms of college or the future. College was something that we would get to some day but we lived in the present, and the dream of playing for our high school team was everything. We never really dwelled on our heroes and idols because the game, and just being a kid, took up too much of our time and was simply too much fun.

Far too many people today spend far too much time trying to be something or someone that they're not. People today have a tendency to judge themselves by how they stack up to others, or to some misconception of importance. Do we own the most expensive car and home in the neighborhood? Are our kids outfitted in the name brands that are "chic" by today's standards? Does our obsession with acceptance take away from our sense of value, and are we teaching these inconsequential values to our youth? Kids today need to be able to look inside themselves and to be grateful for the things they "do" have, instead of dwelling on the things they "want" to have.

People, in today's world, often mistake idol worship for hero worship. Idolizing someone, because they can hit a golf ball three hundred yards or dunk a basketball behind their head, is nothing more than wishful thinking. Though we may dream of accomplishing such feats, more often than not our physical limitations will prevail and deny us the glorified result. Through T.V. and the media we marvel at professional athletes, politicians, actors and actresses, and millionaire tycoons. We fantasize about what it would be like to walk in their shoes and to share in their fame and fortune. There is nothing wrong with a small amount of idol worship. We owe ourselves a little dreaming to take us away from our hectic schedules, but we cannot allow these dreams to become our masters, and idols cannot take the place of true heroes.

The dictionary defines hero as "a person admired for their achievements and qualities." I personally like that word *quality* because it reveals much more than just physical and material accomplishments. I rather think of qualities being tied to components like integrity, compassion, truthfulness, caring, and moral convictions—

the qualities of which true heroes are made. Heroes are those very special people who have had an honest and infallible impact on our lives.

Most of the great motivational and inspirational speakers today start off their talks by giving thanks to those special people who were heroes in their lives. Maybe it was a grandmother who raised them, or a teacher or coach who had a lasting impact in their lives by taking the time to see they walked the straight and narrow.

I personally like to hear speakers who pay tribute to their fathers and mothers. It's heartwarming to hear a grown man or woman recognize their parents as the ones who have had the greatest influence on their lives. Being a parent myself, I can understand how easy it can be to make the mistake of getting so caught up in our children's lives that we lose sight of the fact that it is their lives and not ours.

Parents today have a tendency to control too many aspects of their children's lives, and it is most prevalent in the field of sports. Kids today are often subject to strict schedules with little time set aside for just being a kid. A father, seeing some kid playing basketball, immediately forces his son or daughter to get out on the court, for fear that the kid playing will get ahead of them. Parents are all too often seen carrying their own score books to games in order to keep their own kids' stats. If their child is not the high scorer or playing the position they feel is right for him or her, then there is often an adult showdown over the matter and, more likely than not, it is in front of their children. As I've mentioned earlier, you can pick up any newspaper from around the country and find a story of parents fighting in bleachers, or stories of assault charges, or displays of anger over children's sports that have led to outright riots.

How do children feel when they see their "heroes" displaying such behavior? How can we tell our kids to go out there and have fun and practice sportsmanship when we, as adults, cannot control our own behavior at the cost of their game? As parents, we have to take a step back and view how our kids view us. We owe it to them. We owe them heroes of whom they can be proud. I can think of no greater tribute than to have a son or daughter tell you that they are proud of you. To have a child say thank you for being a positive role model is something special. Parents need to sit down and listen to their children. They need to seriously try to put themselves in their children's shoes and take the time to understand how their children feel about the issues that are affecting their lives. The generation gap today is getting wider, and it's not because our kids are alienating themselves from us, but rather we, as adults, and maybe without our knowledge, are the one's doing the alienating.

I have a tendency to go off on this topic, mainly because the two greatest heroes in my own life were my parents. My mother was simply my best friend. The long talks that we shared, and the warmth and understanding she always showed made me realize there was always going to be someone there for me. There was never a generation gap between myself and my mother; she simply would not allow it. She always wanted to know what was going on in my life, and if I didn't choose to tell her, she had that way, that only mothers can, of finding out. Not because she wanted to dominate my life, but because she wanted us to be close, and we were. It may sound strange by today's standards but even in my college days when I was home for vacation and heading out at night with my friends I would always say to her, "Mom, how about waiting up for me and we can have a talk when I get home," and she always did. To this day, I believe those late night talks with my best friend have made me a better man, a better parent, and a better human being.

There was a tribute given to mothers that I once read that exemplified my mom. It was about the Good Lord creating mothers and the ingredients He needed to mix together to complete the finished product. According to God, she had to have moveable parts and be able to run on black coffee, have a kiss that can cure everything, six pair of hands and three pair of eyes so she wouldn't miss anything. She had to be able to reason and compromise, feed a family on a pound of hamburger, and give you that look, when something is terribly wrong, that says "I know and I still love you".

Heroes come in all shapes and sizes. They can be found in newspaper articles, in human interest stories and on television. All of us watched our New York City heroes on 9/11, wearing police and fire uniforms; risk their lives going into burning buildings to save their fellow Americans. Heroes are found in the workplace, the classroom, and in the political sector. They're found in neighborhoods, in playgrounds, and in churches of every denomination.

Growing up in a small town did not diminish the number of heroes we encountered. There's something to be said about the close-knit small town communities. The town that I grew up in once boomed when the coal industry was at its peak. We lived in the same house where my Dad was born and where he lived his entire life. Even though our region's economy suffered drastically when coal was no longer king, it didn't matter to my Dad. There was simply no better place on the face of this earth. Aside from being a doctor and treating most of the children in town he was an active participant in civic organizations, but the one he was most proud of was his role as president of the town Little League for more the twenty years. He simply loved to go up to the Little League park and watch a game. It was his way of relaxing and we always got a play by play of the game upon his return. My Dad often talked about hometowns in his speeches. He used to say a hometown was made up of people who look out for each other. Where, if a man seen walking down the street with a young woman who was young enough to be his daughter chances are it was his daughter. Where people sat on their porches every evening and enjoyed people stopping by to have a chat. Where friendships were solidified in back yards between people who hung laundry on their clothes lines, and where first dates were simply walking your favorite girl home from the soda shop. The last line of one of my Dad's favorite poems best described his feelings.

> Where people live and dream as one
> In church, in school, or mart,
> But hometowns are not made or built,
> you find them in your "heart".

Hometowns and neighborhoods may have been the most defining aspect of our generation. Parents didn't drive their kids everywhere back then because they didn't have to. Kids left home in the morning and returned home for lunch and supper. There was no need to worry about what we were doing, because the neighborhood had its own set of eyes that kept watch on all of us. Any kid's mother had the right to yell at you if you misbehaved. And the hot line between parents was always answered around supper time when the whole family sat down to eat. Doors were never locked, and sleepovers were a part of our culture. Parents seldom knew who would descend the steps for breakfast the next morning, and the words please and thank you were mandatory in every household.

The little things in life were so important back then, and

our hometowns provided all that was needed. To hang out at the local pizza parlor on a Friday night after a game was something you looked forward to all week. To shoot a game of pool at the local pool room was part of the weekly routine. To catch a Saturday night movie and sit in the balcony of the only movie theater in town was a weekend ritual, and it really didn't matter what flick was playing. To walk to school every day with your best friends, to dance every slow dance at the armory dances, to never miss a holiday parade, and to know exactly what time you needed to get to the playground for fear of not getting picked for the first game, simply was a way of life. Those of you out there who have done all of the above, and I'm sure that most of you from my generation have, take a look in the nearest mirror as you reminisce about those wonderful times and those wonderful places and check out that smile on your face.

As my mother was my best friend growing up, my Dad was my true hero. I learned more lessons from my Dad than I could possibly write down. He taught by example always instilling in me the belief that good things come to good people. Being a pediatrician, his life was devoted to caring for others and his love for children was never denied to his own four kids. My Dad was simply a great role model. Not because of the things he said but because of the way he lived his life.

I remember being with him one day when a man commented about his receding hair line. (My Dad was actually bald at a very young age). I always find it amusing how some simple things can remain with you forever and my Dad's answer to the comment is one of those. His response was, "As long as I have my eyes, my arms, my legs, and my heart, they can take all the hair they want."

My Dad was a great after-dinner speaker. He claimed it was his hobby but it was more like his passion. He often started his speeches with a little poem titled, *I'm Proud To Be An American*, which he was, and he would always end his talks with a simple statement that he took from the entertainer Andy Williams, "May each day of your week be a good day, may the Lord always watch over you" which he meant. My Dad never turned down the opportunity to speak at a local sports banquet or social club function. He loved to tell stories, and he had that great ability to make the audience laugh one minute and bring tears to their eyes the next.

My Dad stood just a little over five feet tall, but to me he was a giant of a man. When I talk about a person's journey to success, I often think of my Dad as being the most successful man that I've ever known. Not in terms of achieving greatness or financial stability, but rather in his attitude and approach to his every day life, and his uncanny ability to touch the lives of so many others.

I hope I speak for all the fathers out there when I say, "It should be our dream to have our children look up to us and respect us." Is there a greater feeling in the world than to have your child give you a hug and kiss before he or she

WHEN THE GAME WAS JUST A GAME

goes off to bed or to hear them say those precious words, "Dad, I love you?"

Parents today need to be heroes to their children. We, as parents, can't try to live our lives through our kids. They deserve a chance to be the best they can be. We need to learn to be supportive in whatever they pursue, and we need to be the type of role model they can be proud of.

Young people do not have exclusive rights to heroes. Heroes can be found in our adult lives as well. As I've said, heroes can come in all shapes and sizes, and if we take the time to look we can even find them in the youth of today. I'm not talking about kids who are great athletes or child stars, but rather young people who, because of certain circumstances, have opened our eyes to the important things in life and have made our world a little more positive, and maybe even made us better adults for having crossed our paths.

There was a young man I had the great pleasure of teaching quite a few years ago, that I still consider one of my heroes. My first recollection of Michael was that of a skinny little freshman, who made his way down the corridor of the high school with a peculiar way of walking. I learned soon after that Michael suffered from a disease called Muscular Dystrophy. Michael's awkward gait often made it difficult for him to carry books and supplies, and it was not uncommon to see him looking a bit unorganized on his journey to and from class.

Regardless of the difficulties, Michael always did get to class, and he was diligent to get his assignments completed. By the end of his freshman year it became common knowledge that here was a kid with a driving determination. Michael wasn't without his doubters, however. Adults were often heard singing his praises but questioning whether or not he would be able to continue through the remainder of his high school years. Some wondered whether he'd even be strong enough to return as a sophomore. Michael did make his return to school as a tenth-grader, to the surprise of these skeptics. In his second year he was confined to a wheel chair. The wheel chair may have taken some of Michael's burdens away, though his life as a high school student was far from the norm. Michael still had trouble transporting books which he carried on his lap, and even the simplest task of hanging up his coat in his locker often required several tries. It was not uncommon to see him pop into class a few minutes after the bell rang, and all of his teachers did take that into consideration.

Late for class or not, Michael always seemed to find the resolve to get his assignments completed. His determination and fortitude was a model for his classmates regardless of the physical difficulties he endured. He seldom was seen without his infectious smile gracing his face. After Michael's sophomore year the doubters once again questioned whether or not he would have the strength to return for his junior year. Sure enough, the following September Michael was present with the rest of his classmates, but this time with a motorized wheel chair to lessen the load even more and make school life a little easier for him. Still, every day was a challenge and through it all Michael persevered.

Being a school teacher, you sometimes have to bite your lip and control your emotions at statements made throughout the course of a school day. One such instance happened to me during Michael's junior year. Being a coach at the time, I happened to be walking through the gymnasium one day while class was in progress. I couldn't help noticing Michael sitting in his wheel chair in the corner of the gym watching his classmates go through their exercises. Michael was not obligated to attend gym class. He could have spent the period in the library or computer room, but he chose to attend class with his peers regardless of not being able to participate. On this particular day I happened to notice three boys sitting in the bleachers, not participating. I stopped to ask the three why they were not taking class, and I was answered, at first, with a few snickers. One of the boys finally said, "I forgot my sneakers," to which the others found amusing. The other two followed up by saying, "We didn't feel like taking gym today so we told the teacher that we didn't feel well." After my rage subsided and I collected myself, I said to the three, "I wonder what it would be like, if for just one day that young man sitting down there in that wheel chair could get up and take gym class. I wonder if he would forget his sneakers or fake being sick." Through my disgust I looked at the three of them and told them that he probably would not be able to sleep the night before anticipating the excitement of being able to use his legs even for a short time.

Getting back to Michael's journey, he completed his junior year and once again his doubters commented on his perseverance, but questioned his chances of graduating the following year. Michael put all doubt to rest as he returned his senior year, with a determination that could be seen on his face day in and day out. Still showing up for classes a little late, still struggling with simple tasks that we all take for granted, and still going through his school day with that smile on his face, made us all a little more aware of our own good fortunes. By now I'm sure you realize that Michael did graduate that spring, but the most amazing thing happened to me the night of his graduation. As I watched Michael head to the stage, in his wheel chair, to receive his diploma, I realized that I was in the presence of a hero whose passion for life would stay with me for a long time. And I can still remember standing there, with tears running down my face, as the superintendent read his name and, through the applause from the audience, announce that Michael will graduate *Number Two* in this year's senior class.

I've told Michael's story more times than I can remember. I like to remind kids and adults that they are blessed with so many gifts that are often taken for granted. I tell them not only to look for heroes in their lives but to strive to be heroes. Mariah Carey ends one of my favorite songs with the words, "A Hero Lies in You". Think about it! Remember it every time that son or daughter strikes out or misses a breakaway lay-up. Remember it every time their eyes fill up with tears because they feel that they may have let you down. Remember it when others turn their backs on them or when they suffer from that first broken heart. Remember just how absolutely wonderful they are. BE A HERO!

# EXCUSES

# EXCUSES

It's easy to quit when the going gets tough
It's easy to turn and just go
It's easy to say that I've had quite enough
When you face that unyielding foe

Why am I concerned what the outcome may show
Is it all that important to me
Why not just give in and say I don't care
And accept that whatever will be

I can't and I won't, I don't care what they say
It's so easy to give up the fight
To make my excuse and to think it's okay
And believe what I'm doing is right

But am I content when each day is at end
When I look in the mirror and say
Did I give it my all, did I give it my best
Or again did I fake it today

For excuses are there, they can always be found
With some searching you'll find that denial
But to those who refuse to give in to their hold
You're the ones who will sleep with a smile

—dah

The large number of kids dropping out of sports today may be of little importance with respect to the more pressing issues facing our society. However, if young people give up on dreams before they're old enough to know how great those dreams can be, then what happens when they are faced with the real challenges life has to offer? Do they become the next gencration of excuse makers and pass the trait on to their children, and so on and so forth?

I like dreamers. I believe in them, and I believe without them we become stagnant. One of my favorite stories is Cervantes *Don Quixote*. If you've never read the book or seen the stage show or movie "Man of La Mancha", make it a point to do so; you owe it to yourself. It's the story of an old, senile man who, with a faithful companion, sets out to right the wrongs of the world. It's the simple and sincere life of a dreamer who can't help but touch your heart. I'm not suggesting that people today should live their lives in the clouds, but dreams are from what all great accomplishments in life were nurtured.

I have a very good friend who today is a college basketball coach at a very prestigious university. Over the years I've heard him speak at numerous camps, and he always ends his talks with the same message. He tells kids that they should, "dream dreams and have the courage and commitment to make those dreams come true." He is a living example of what can be accomplished with hard work, imagination, and a dream.

I mentioned earlier that I grew up in a small coal mining town in Northeastern Pennsylvania. By the 1960's, most of the coal mines were shut down and most of the coal breakers (also known as collieries) were left standing, a reminder to those who viewed them of a time when coal was king. The population of many of the towns in our region has decreased rapidly from this boom period. We've had trouble attracting new industries, but it has never dampened the spirit of our people. The resolve of many of the old timers and the work ethic they instilled in their children is something in which to be proud. There's a certain mystique associated with these people and there's a statement that describes them best:

"Tough times made tough people". These are the kind of people on which our country was built. People who asked nothing more than to be paid an honest wage for an honest day's work.

I'm sad to say that society today has lost some of this attitude. I'm tired of listening to people who are excuse makers. I'm tired of people living their lives consumed with the belief that life owes them something, or that there's a magic potion out there that will insure their happiness. Millions of dollars are poured into lottery picks, cosmetic surgery, and the latest weight loss phenomenon. People spend hours each day complaining about their jobs, their fellow workers, and their bosses. Many people simply love to be miserable, and they pass the trait on to anyone who wants to listen, and more damaging is the fact that this attitude is being passed down to the youth of today.

I use to give a homework assignment to my students on a Friday called "TGIM" which stood for *Thank God Its Monday*. Their objective was to wake up on Monday morning and be the most positive person they could possibly be. They were to make breakfast for a member of their family, be nice to their brothers and sisters and be outright pleasant regardless of those around them embracing the "Monday morning blues." When they made it to my class on Monday morning we would discuss their findings. You can't imagine some of the reports and responses that were brought to the table. Some kids talk about parents asking them, "What is the matter with you, are you on something?" Others said people told them to shut up and stop smiling. Others said it was outright funny how people looked at them and walked away. All because of a particular day of the week!

Spending more than half of my life as a teacher, I've seen a steady change in the attitudes of young people. I know you're probably thinking, "Here's one of those teachers who constantly reminds students what it was like when he was young." Wrong! I don't believe kids have changed, other than the fads and the music that has represented every generation. What I am saying is that more kids make excuses today when faced with tough decisions, because our society has told them that it's okay to do so.

What ever happened to people who actually liked their jobs? How strange is it today to see an employee do a little extra without being compensated for it? I used to hear my Dad talk about the men who worked the mines. He often told us how he remembered, as a young boy, seeing these men, many who were immigrants struggling with the English language, walking to work each day with smiles on their faces, men who were thankful to have a job and grateful to be living in America. Women who worked at the same machine in the same factory and took pride in the fact that they seldom missed a day were the stereotype. These were people who possessed a work ethic that for some reason has been dwindling in today's society. People back then were not categorized by their language or nationality but by their integrity and drive.

I recently heard about a conference, attended by some of my colleagues, where a gentleman with a doctorate in education made the following statement, "By the second grade all students should have some idea of their future plans and should be grouped accordingly." He said that kids should have a cluster or range of job ideas in direct correlation to their intelligence.

I constantly listen to politicians' debate accountability of students based solely on standardized test scores and national standards. Seldom is the phrase, "work ethic" ever used in regards to the achievement of our youth. We live in the greatest country in the world, built by people like the miners and the factory workers who were willing to work hard, day in and day out. People took care of their children and raised them with a set of values, one being an honest day's work for an honest day's pay. These were people who did not base their child's development on standards, or test scores, or clusters projecting their future. It was a time when excuses would not be tolerated and a time nurtured by a patriotic belief that anyone could achieve anything if they were willing to work for it. It's time that we allowed dreams to come back into this hectic world we live in since dreams are, and always will be, the only basis for real achievement.

I received an e-mail at school one day, re-enforcing my belief of how today's society gets caught up, way too much, in its own problems and tends to lose sight of the big picture. The e-mail was from a marketing group, and it was one of those stories that you were asked to read and forward to as many people as you can in the span of fifteen minutes. Like many of you, when I receive these letters, I have a tendency to bypass or simply delete them, believing they are a waste of my time, but this particular story caught my eye. Since I've read it, I have become a little more patient and observant to what crosses my computer screen. The story was about a man who was returning home from a business trip only to find that the jet he was flying on was, for some unknown reason, delayed. The man was anxious to get home after a long trip and his patience was shot. Frustrated, he began to thumb through the Sky Mall magazine hoping that the flight would soon be underway. When the passengers were finally seated the cabin door still did not close and no one seemed to be in any hurry to get the plane off the ground even though they were well past the scheduled takeoff time. As frustration continued to build within the man the flight attendants voice came over the intercom announcing that the plane was being held for some very special people. The man was expecting some celebrity or sports figure to be the reason and only wished that they would just get on the plane so everyone could be on their way. The attendant at that point announced that they were being joined by several United States Marines who were returning from Iraq. As the marines walked on board, the plane erupted in applause. The men were taken by surprise by the 300 plus passengers cheering for them. The passengers were shaking the soldiers' hands and reaching out to just touch a part of their uniforms as they filed down the aisle in search of their seats. The man recalled when they were finally airborne, that he had to take a few minutes to examine his conscience. He considered his goal of getting home to an easy chair, a cold drink, and a remote control but put those thoughts aside considering what these men had done for all of us. He talked about taking for granted the everyday freedoms we possess and the conveniences of the American way of living and that we forget that others have paid a price for our ability to complain. The story ends with the man requesting to the flight attendant to keep everyone seated upon landing to allow these heroes to exit first. He admitted that he felt a sense of pride and was honored to be among the first to welcome these heroes home. The man vowed that he would never forget that flight or the lesson he learned from it.

There's no hiding from the fact that wc live in a society of excuse makers. Everyone wants to be richer, or better looking, or taller, or shorter, or thinner, or more popular, and the list goes on and on. It seems like it's easier to hide behind excuses than it is to stand up and face the realities and challenges that life has to offer. There are more lawyers today willing to back up our excuses than ever before. People today are being sued left and right. Don't slip on someone's pavement or you'll be sued. Don't tell a joke in the workplace that may offend a fellow employee or you'll be sued. Be careful what you say to your students or even to your children or you'll be sued. We have people in our society suing each other for every reason imaginable. People are suing cigarette companies because they smoke. They're suing fast food restaurants because their children are over-weight. They're suing coffee shops because their coffee is too hot. People are more concerned with their rights than they are with what's right. People are suing doctors, and the escalating malpractice insurance rates are causing doctors to relocate to areas where they can afford to practice their profession. On this matter, I can't speak for anyone else, but if I'm going to have a brain operation I'm making it a point to reassure my surgeon that no matter what the outcome, he or she doesn't have to worry about a lawsuit. The last thing I want is to be lying on a table with my head open and having the surgeon's hand shaking for fear of a lawsuit if he or she messes up.

A generation ago things just didn't seem as complicated. I have to laugh thinking about my Dad in terms of malpractice. As I mentioned earlier, we lived across the street from our grade school playground. It was a common occurrence for a kid to take an elbow to the eye or mouth that might require stitches and to see that kid walk across the street and take a seat in the waiting room until my Dad could fit him in and tend to his needs. More often than not the kid would return to the playground and finish the game, and my Dad would get a call later in the evening from the parents of the boy thanking him and asking him what they owed. There were no forms to be filled out or accident reports to be filed, and there were no lawsuits brought against the kid who threw the elbow or the school that owned the playground. The situation would be taken care of, and the kids were always back playing the next day no worse for wear.

Have extra-curricular activities suffered due to excuses ranging from bad coaching to poor preparation to lack of funding? Are athletes today accountable for how hard they work in practice, or how much time they spend working on their game in the off season? It seems that, in most sports, as soon as the starting team is picked, it's time for those who are not chosen as one of the elite group to make excuses as to why they're not included. It's never their fault, and all too often they quit, justifying their departure with that well known phrase, "I got screwed".

Adults need to realize they are the ones who hold the key. Enabling children to make excuses at the expense of their coaches can only cause harm. Kids need to be made aware that excuses are a dime a dozen and get them nowhere.

# THE GIRLS

# GIRLS

Girls in the game
How can it be so
Too small and too weak
Too frail and too slow

Too pretty to handle
The game down inside
Too dainty, too meek
We'll just take it in stride

When did it all change
What force did they sway
What gave them the skills
What taught them the way

It happened so fast
They made it look fun
They learned how to pass,
How to jump, shoot, and run

They're part of it now
They're in for the ride
They play it for keeps
There's nowhere to hide

And I'm glad they're a part
For the game doesn't flex
It's a challenge to all
Doesn't matter what sex

So girls do your thing
And show others the way
You've made skeptics believe
Because "Boy Can You Play"

—dah

Please do not believe for one minute that I would bypass the girl's game. Women's basketball has witnessed an amazing boom over the past twenty-five years. The professional game has produced stars like Lisa Leslie and Cynthia Cooper. Television coverage and endorsements have helped to promote the women's pro league. The women's college game skyrocketed into national prominence in the 1970's when little Immaculata College from the suburbs of Philadelphia won the national title to a sixty-four team tournament, with the likes of U-Conn and Tennessee battling with other top programs in front of packed houses on national T.V. Filtering down, the high school girls' game, in some areas, has outsold the boys' games at the ticket booths, and many of today's high school female players have become local heroes with the coffee shop and watering hole fans of their respective areas.

Unfortunately for the girls, they have not escaped the pressures and demands that have grown along with the popularity of the sport. In fact, the ascension of the girls' game, in such a short time, has raised the level of expectation to the point of damaging the game itself. It may be true that we are not seeing the early exits from college or the high school star bypassing her college career to enter the professional ranks, but can it be far off? Exposure camps, weekend shootouts, and AAU tournaments are all on equal terms with the boys. Youth leagues and practice demands on young girls are surpassing the boys in terms of preparation and hours spent.

I read an article in a local newspaper advertising a tryout for an AAU team. The article read, "Looking to form a ten and under girl's team, must be committed and willing to travel." I personally have a hard time believing any child knows whether or not they're committed to anything when they are less than ten years old. What I read into this advertisement is how many parents of girls under ten are committed and willing to travel. A few of the older girls I've had the privilege of interviewing played on these early AAU squads when they were young, and they admitted it was fun traveling to different cities, staying in hotel rooms, and meeting new friends, but they all said that the novelty wore off as they got a little older. Some said that if they knew then what they know now they wouldn't have started playing with these traveling squads at such a young age. They also admitted the pressure to win and to play well seemed to intensify with each year of involvement. Some believe that the burnout rate increases due to the number of games played and to the amount of travel involved. Are adults really looking out for the best interests of their kids by convincing them that traveling every weekend is best for them? Is the commitment in time and money benefiting a child, or is it fulfilling the need and the ego of those in charge?

Weight training, which at one time was solely for the purpose of producing bigger and stronger male players, has become mandatory in the development of girls' programs from college to high school and even younger. Injuries to women in sports are skyrocketing. More girls are being sidelined for sports related injuries than ever before, and careers are ending at younger and younger ages. The American Academy of Orthopedic Surgeons, in recent studies, reported that female soccer and basketball players are three to four times more likely to tear their ACL than males. The majority of these injuries are occurring in women between the ages of fifteen and twenty-five. Could the rising epidemic of ACL tears among women basketball players have anything to do with the more up-tempo and physical style of play that the girls have adopted? Are the longer practice hours and physical demands far surpassing their physical capabilities? I've listened to physiologists talk about the maturing process of women and the probability of greater risk to knee injuries due to body structure. I'm sure on the professional and college level the girls are equipped and monitored with much more consistency, but what about the high school female athlete? Should the girls and coaches be better educated in terms of sports injuries or will the numbers continue to rise?

Aside from injuries, will the number of young girls participating in the game begin to diminish due to the pressure? Will the girls start to drop out of the sport at younger and younger ages, for fear of not measuring up to early expectations? Some believe the process has already begun, and others believe that it is far beyond help already.

I came to be a fan of the girl's game in recent years mainly because I have a couple of nieces who participated at the high school level. I applaud the strides the girl's game has made in such a relatively short time. Being a high school teacher, I've noticed a common bond that has developed between the male and the female athletes of the high school. Athletic bonding, years ago, was solely tied to just the male players, and I'm glad to see it bridge the gender gap. There seems to be a new found respect between the girl and boy athletes of most schools, and I feel that it's not only great in terms of school spirit but also a positive, in that it fosters knew friendships and breaks down old stereotypes.

A few years back, I was coaching the boy's team, and we were having a pretty good season. Our girl's, likewise, were in the playoff hunt and enjoying a banner year. I remember one night, when getting ready to face our biggest rival, seeing the whole girl's team enter the gym wearing funny outfits and then leading the cheers in the middle of our cheering section in support of our boys. What I did not know was that the night before when our girl's were playing the same rival school my boy's team did the very same thing. Another year I recall our girls playing for a state title, and I was amazed and very proud of the male athletes of our school, not just the basketball players, who took it upon themselves to decorate the school in the girls' honor. Seldom is there jealousy between the girls' and boys' programs, and I've actually witnessed some lasting relationships develop between some of the male and female athletes of our school.

I have to admit that my generation's view of girl's sports was different. The popularity of the girl's game actually did not catch on until organization took over and, for that, I feel a little sorry for today's female players. You'll seldom hear reference made to days of pickup games and playground friendships. Ask about their earliest recollection of the game and most girls will go back to their first organized team. Ask about playing just for the fun of it, even though their love for the game is without question and most cannot recall every playing the game, even as a youth without some form of organizational backing.

I've had the opportunity to interview a number of female players who played at the high school and the college levels. I asked all concerned the same question, "What is the biggest drawback to the girl's game today?" Most agreed that the pressures and expectations have gotten way out of hand. Many focused on AAU teams they got involved with early. Most agreed that when they started to play on these elite teams their initial goal was simply to get better, but as time went on the pressure and the obsession with a college scholarship took away a lot of the fun. Some said they made some great friendships regardless and, in itself, it was a positive experience. Additionally, many agreed these friendships were often strained because the game was not as important as the individual play, a stress brought on entirely by parents. I was told by one of the girls, who was a high school player, that a teammate of hers was not allowed to play with her high school team throughout the summer for fear that she might suffer an injury and not be able to compete in exposure tournaments. Another story was of a high school girl who was told if she did not perform well in a particular tournament she would not be allowed to use the car for a week. I talked to a coach of an elite team who years before played at a Division I school herself. She confided in me there were times when she wanted to tell some of these demanding parents that instead of pushing for a free college ride they should hope their daughters do not get scholarships, knowing the demands placed on college athletes today.

Parents need to put their child's best interest at hand before they commit them to something that might be over their heads and downright damaging. I recently talked to the father of a young girl who played for an elite team as a fourth grader. The father has a basketball background himself, and although he was skeptical, based on reports he had heard, he allowed his daughter to join the team. He said the experience at first was positive. His daughter was meeting new friends, and the practices and games were fun. His daughter talked about her team constantly, and he was convinced he made the right decision.

At first, everyone on the team was playing the same amount of time, and there didn't seem to be too much emphasis placed on winning and losing. The problems, he said, started when the team really began to do well, and the tournaments they were entering were getting a little more competitive. He said he could not believe the intensity level of parents in the stands at some of these games. One father who was sitting behind him at a game was not only screaming at his own daughter but calling her a bum. Keep in mind that we're talking about nine and ten-year-old girls. Although his feelings were starting to change, he continually asked his daughter if she was still having fun, and on her assurance he allowed her to stay on the team even though he was doubtful it was best for her.

He said the straw that broke the camel's back came when the team qualified for a national tournament. Once they arrived at the tournament the atmosphere completely changed. Coaches started to believe they had a chance of winning it all. The idea of equal time was a thing of the past and even though his daughter was getting a generous amount of playing time, he found himself embarrassed for those kids who were not. He said that coaches, not only of his daughter's team but of the majority of teams involved, were prancing up and down the sidelines, screaming at referees and chastising their players without mercy. He said it got to a point where he actually considered removing his daughter from the floor. He confided in me that when the tournament finally ended he took his daughter aside and told her not to judge the game of basketball by what took place here. He stated he only wished he could have erased much of it from her memory, but knowing he could not, he vowed it would never happen again. He told me from that moment until she is in high school, if she still enjoys the game, she will only play in her respective league, and he will have a say as to who coaches her and how that coach will handle the game and the players involved.

This obsession with the almighty scholarship has taken on knew meaning with regard to the girls' game. Parents rank tournaments and camps strictly by the degree of exposure their daughters will get. Tryouts for elite teams bring in players from far-off destinations. The amount of travel to games and to practice sites does not seem to be a factor to parents, if the ultimate goal can be achieved.

I've interviewed some girls who reached the pinnacle of success by capturing the college scholarship. I must admit I actually felt sorry for some of them, after listening to their stories and wondering if it was really worth it. Some admitted that they completely lost interest in the game, in that they have been playing it competitively since fourth grade. Other commented on playing out their scholarship and never wanting to pick up a basketball again.

Elite teams and high expectations are not the only pressures facing the women players of today. With its rise in popularity, high school girls' basketball carries with it a sense of community awareness like never before. I talked with a few of the local high school players, and they said they have a hard time dealing with the phonies who project themselves as fans, the ones who are always around, sitting in the front row of every game and patting them on the back when they win. They believe these are the same bleacher bums who are constantly spreading rumors about them off the court, and the ones who turn on them as soon as things go bad. This type of fair-weather fan is someone to whom the boys' game may have grown accustomed, but to the girls it may be something new. I was actually surprised when one of the female players said it was something that really bothered her and caused her to be cautious around people outside of the game. It made me realize that the girls' game is still evolving, and it may carry more negative baggage with it than the boys' game ever did.

The area in which I live is really a hotbed for girls' high school basketball. We've had at least six schools over the last twenty-five years who not only competed in, but won, state championships; some of the schools more than once. I had the opportunity to sit down with some of the coaches from these great programs, and I asked for their perspectives as to where the girls' game is today and where it might be heading.

Ron Rhen was a high school teacher at Pine Grove Area High School for thirty-six years, seventeen of which he also served as the athletic director. Ron coached high school girls' basketball for thirty-one years, compiling a record of 675 wins and 170 losses. During his coaching tenure his teams won twelve league championships, thirteen district championships and two state championships. Ron is, to say the least, a legend in our area, as well as in our entire state.

Ron Rhen is a true pioneer of the girls' game. He remembers when he first started coaching the girls. They were still playing with six players. He also recalls the early days when there were not enough high school referees to do both boys and girls games and how they would have to recruit high school boy players to officiate the girls' J.V. games. Ron believes it was the change from six players to five that revolutionized the girls' game. "Once the girls were allowed to run the floor and play with the same rules as the boys, the girls' game just took off." Ron laughs at the thought of outside interference back in the early days. "Very few parents attended games back then, and there was no support at all from the student body. It didn't take long however before a few girls started to dedicate themselves to the sport, and once they did the rest was history." Ron admits that Title 9 was also a major stepping stone, due to the fact that it insured a commitment, by the powers in charge, to bring the girls' game into the interscholastic framework.

When asked about the girls' game today, and where it might be heading, Ron believes like so many others of a generation past, that way too much pressure is being placed on players, and expectations are getting out of control. "Parents especially need to be toned down. There needs to be a survey conducted and made available as to how many girls actually make it to the college level. Parents need to realize the fact that it is unlikely that their daughters will ever play beyond high school. They need to allow their girls to play and enjoy the sport for what it is and for the time they have to play it." Ron also believes that organization in the sport starts way too early. Third and fourth grade girls should not be placed in leagues where winning and losing becomes important. Girls are burning out faster than ever before.

It's no wonder that, with Title 9 and other advancements in women's sports, the game has taken on greater importance. I am not knocking girls' basketball since, as I said earlier, I have truly become a fan. My fear is, as with so many other areas of our game, the girl's game will eventually suffer. Young girls will begin, and I'm not sure it hasn't already started, to look elsewhere. Will it get to the point where the game will no longer be a game, and the players will no longer be players but commodities? Will young girls start dropping out long before they realize how great a game it can be? Those involved need to take a long, hard look, and those girls who grew up with the game need to take it upon themselves to teach the young players about the positives associated with the game.

Is there hope for the future? Definitely! I recently read an article about a girls alumni game played for a very worthwhile charity at North Schuylkill High School in Northeastern Pennsylvania. A local television station was running a campaign called "Stuff the Truck" in support of the troops who were fighting the war in Iraq. Instead of buying a ticket to the alumni game, patrons were asked to donate items such as wet wipes, stationery paper and other useful products that could be sent to our soldiers. Careen Caufield, the young woman responsible for the event, was a former standout player as well as the former coach of that high school girls' team. Careen launched the annual game three years prior to this event for the purpose of bringing some former players back together and to raise money to benefit a different charity each year. From its initial start it has grown in popularity and has become a traditional spring homecoming.

The girls' basketball program of North Schuylkill High School has been a very successful one. In fact, the article lists it as having one of the great traditions in Pennsylvania sports. The gymnasium is filled with banners paying tribute to league, district, and state championships. A long list of thousand point scorers, All-State recognitions, and girls who continued their career at the next level, are testaments to its excellence.

Thirty ex-players returned for this year's game, many traveling from out of state to attend the festivities. All the participants wore shirts with their names on the back and a picture of the American flag on the front. Their were two pictures accompanying the newspaper article, one showing a player sporting a incredible smile playing with the ten month old child of one of the other girls during a time-out. The second picture showed one of the players holding her two terrier dogs during the half-time break. I thought it ironic that neither picture was centered on the game itself but rather on the occasion, and I commend the writer and the photographer for portraying the sport at one of its finest moments. Unless one has played the game at a competitive level or been involved with a group of friends who are committed to the same goal, it may be difficult to understand why a mother might give up a weekend for the sake of playing in a basketball game. The special friendships and the love and respect for the game are something that only they can deem worthwhile.

I must say that I admire those women who return for this wonderful event each year, and my hat goes off to Careen Caufield for her commitment to its continuation. I also breathe a sigh of relief that the love of the game, and possibly the future of the game, will be in good hands if there are other schools and programs around the country doing similar things. It's up to all of the women who have played the game and still look at it as a "great game", to educate the young players who are coming up. I urge you to remind them how great the game can be. How the camaraderie, the competition, the respect, and the feeling of accomplishment, can have such a positive impact on their lives. Impress upon the young players of today that basketball is not all about championships, scholarships, and prestige, but rather about the friendships that can last a lifetime and bridge time-zones. We need to make them aware of all the good things that can come out of the game long after the ball stops bouncing.

# BASKETBALL

B—is for baskets, the ones that go in
A—is for assists, they always help you win
S—is for steals, for it's defense we play
K—is to keep it, don't throw it away
E—is for excitement, like no other game
T—is for teamwork, we're one and the same
B—is for all of the teams that you'll beat
A—is for all of the friends that you'll meet.
L—is for living and for learning the way
L—is for loving This Game That We Play!

—dah

# REPUTATION

# RULES OF REPUTATION

If you follow your heart, you're heading in the right
direction.
Do the right thing even though it may not be the
popular thing.
Be the first to class every day.
Do you own homework. Copying someone else's is a
copout.
Treat others—adults, peers, and those less fortunate—
with respect.
Be judged by your actions, not by your words.
Don't be satisfied with results, strive to do better.
Be a leader in your own way and in your own mind
Popularity is not as important as productivity
Be truly thankful for what you have

—dah

If there are so many negatives associated with the game today, if the psychological effects are harmful to our youth, if the pressures and expectations placed on young athletes are getting out of hand, then why would we ever want our children to play? I believe, and I'm sure I speak for many others, that sports can be a wonderful learning experience for those involved. The true nature of athletics should manifest itself around becoming a team player, enjoying sports as an extra-curricular, and benefiting from lessons that go along with winning and losing. And lest we not forget that all involved, especially those in their early years, should first and foremost be having fun. I truly believe players take pride in their accomplishments and in the fact they are athletes. Lessons in humility, integrity, dignity and hard work will be carried with them long after the games are over.

Two words that have become the cornerstones for most of my banquet and camp talks are reputation and determination. I constantly tell young athletes that the most powerful word in the English language is reputation. Reputation is defined as "a general or public estimation of someone or something, the state of being highly regarded or esteemed." I try to emphasize to our youth the reason the word carries such merit is because it is the only word in the English language that individuals have 100% control of. I tell them that their reputation is not dependent on their parents, teachers, coaches, teammates, or friends. Though many of those mentioned can have an impact on it, only they themselves have the final say as to how others will view them, and I remind them that they cannot, for one minute, believe what others think is not important.

As a teacher, I often hear kids in the hallways making negative comments about their teachers such as, "I don't care what she thinks of me," "I don't like him anyway, so I'm not working in his class." I listen to kids talk about harassing the bus driver on the way to school and giving the cafeteria lady a hard time while standing in line for lunch. I constantly hear derogatory statements made about fellow classmates. I often remind these kids of a lesson I learned many years ago, and one that has proven to be true more times than not. If people are quick to tell you stories about others then you can bet they are just as quick to tell others stories about you. I remind them that the teachers they are bad mouthing may someday be asked to submit a recommendation for them, that the bus driver or cafeteria worker could some day be their father-in-law or mother-in-law, and the smaller kid that is constantly being picked on and made fun of might one day be the person who is signing their paychecks.

Athletes are always under the microscope. I once heard Coach Jim Calhoun, the great basketball coach from the University of Connecticut, interviewed regarding players actions on and off the court. He said he constantly reminds his players that there is a price to pay for being a college athlete. There's no question, in the eyes of the public, athletes are viewed a little differently, and it's not just at the upper levels of the sport. High school athletes are held accountable to the same criteria. I personally remember one Thursday evening, the night before a big game, when I was a senior in high school hearing my mother answer the phone of an anonymous caller. My Mother was a little alarmed at the severity of the man's tone, so she handed the phone to my Dad. The voice on the other end claimed to be a fan that followed our high school team. He proceeded to tell my father that I was having a great season but with the important game coming up tomorrow there's something that he should know. The voice went on to describe how he just happened to be driving around town, and he couldn't help but notice myself and some of my high school teammates standing up town, and he believed we had been drinking. My Dad asked the man what his name was, and the man would only tell him he was a concerned fan. My Dad, getting a little angry said, "I'd really like to know your name because I'd like to know the liar who's spreading this rumor! You see my son is sitting right here watching television with me." The man immediately hung up.

Is there a bit of jealousy and envy when it comes to high school athletes? Of course there is, and there should be. Athletes should be held to a higher standard because they represent their schools, their families, and their communities as well as themselves. Most high school coaches do outstanding jobs enforcing school policies by seeing to it that their players toe the line. Why is it that so many players at the professional level, the apex of the sport, aren't held to the same standards? Why is the irresponsible behavior in the pro ranks not only accepted but often applauded by so many?

Reputations are difficult to maintain and easy to break down. I constantly remind young athletes that there will always be jealousy aimed at them. I tell them to be prepared for it and to handle it with care. A reputation is important, and it's worth more than the small minds that will try to tear it down. My Dad use to tell a story about an old time college coach who was on the recruiting trail and was asked, What kind of players are you looking for? The coach replied, "I'm looking for *SISSYS*". The man asked him to explain and the coach said,

> "Is it a sissy to be the first one to practice every day and the last one to leave?
>
> Is it a sissy to be thought of as a tough competitor on the court and a gentleman off the court?
>
> Is it a sissy to be seen leaving school every day with your gym bag in one hand and your book bag in the other?
>
> Is it a sissy to put teamwork far ahead of individual accomplishments?
>
> Is it a sissy to believe that it's more important to be judged as a good person than it is to be judged as a  good player?"

The coach went on to say he's always looking for *sissys*. Good players are a dime a dozen, but *sissys* are something special because they're what champions are made of.

Are the majority of players today more concerned with

trash talk and showmanship than they are with the game itself? If so, it's not hard to understand why. The bad boys all too often dominate the headlines and the weekly highlights. Individual performances and plays of the week far surpass team statistics. Seldom will you see a player today extend a hand to help an opponent up after he's been knocked to the floor. Reading the lips of some professional and college coaches during a highly contested contest could have all the grounds for an "R" rating and still the camera follows the controversy. Players, who's off court actions, as well as their tardiness or absence from practices, are much more newsworthy than those *sissys* who happen to show up on time, work hard, and never miss a practice. Why should anyone want to read about them? After all they're only doing what they're being paid to do.

The obvious concern of those who love the game is whether or not this irresponsible behavior is filtering down to the lower levels. Are there still some values left attached to the sport or is sportsmanship a lost entity? I sincerely hope the gym rats of today still have a little *sissy* in them, and I pray the word *reputation* becomes their focal point, both on and off the court.

# ATTITUDE

Maybe it's nothing more than the way we view the big picture, when trying to rationalize the changes that have been implemented into the game of basketball today. Maybe it was just a simpler time and a simpler game a generation ago. We're constantly reminded of how our world is changing and how the bus isn't going to wait for us. It's an attitude that has been forced upon us, and one we have grown to accept.

If it is attitude, then the young people of today need to take the time and asses the meaning of the word *attitude,* and they need to come to the realization that attitude is everything in the world of sports, and pretty much, everything in life. Parents confront it, coaches dwell on it, teachers question it, and jobs often depend on it. Having a good attitude can open doors for you, and it can be the difference between achievement and failure, victory and defeat, health and sickness, and even laughter and tears.

An old story I once read told of an elderly gentleman who lost his wife and whose children seldom visited him. The man lived alone in a modest dwelling and survived on the bare essentials of life. The extraordinary happiness and positive attitude of the man had many questioning his sanity. When asked why he always had a smile on his face and a spring in his step when he actually had so little about which to be cheerful, the man answered, When I wake up in the morning I have one major decision to make before I take my first step, and that is whether to have a good day or a bad day, and every morning I simply make the same decision, and that is to have a good day. Can attitude be that basic? Why not?

People can shape their attitude to fit any circumstances in their lives. Even pain can be a positive, if your attitude decides it should be. Take all the athletes out there who have spent some time relaxing their sore muscles in the sauna or the steam room after a challenging workout. How about those who have installed the Jacuzzi on the outside deck or patio and submerged themselves each evening unwinding from the stress and strain of the workplace. Those of you who dive into a cold swimming pool on a hot summer day after finishing a five mile run have felt it. The Thursday night basketball regulars who venture to their favorite watering hole after seven or eight highly contested pickup games, who after an hour or so, have to struggle to get themselves off the barstool, not because of the cold ones they consumed, but because of the "good soreness" that settles into every well used joint and muscle in their bodies. Is there any greater feeling in the world, physically or mentally, than that total exhaustion brought on by a vigorous workout? Is it an attitude that drives us? Those who think its crazy have never been there; those who have are addicted. The belief that a workout just isn't a workout unless its accompanied by a drenching sweat is an attitude that only the true athlete can comprehend. Those who play that one extra pickup game after their bodies are saying it's time to stop. Those who run that one extra mile or swim that one extra lap in the pool know the feeling.

Joe Muldowny knows the feeling. He's in his mid-fiftees and an avid runner. Joe has been running for more than thirty years and still averages approximately fifty miles a week. He also writes a column for our local newspaper featuring running tips and human interest stories on the history and legends of the sport. Joe still competes, both in and out of his age group, and he can be seen, regardless of the weather or the season, religiously getting in his daily miles around town.

I recently had the opportunity to sit down with Joe, and I asked him why he stays after it and what it is that keeps him going when others, half his age, have thrown the running shoes away:

> "I can't describe the feeling I get when I don't run. When I miss a day I feel like I've cheated myself. About four years ago I broke my ankle and I couldn't get out on the road. It was the worst six weeks of my adult life. I guess I'm somewhat addicted but it's a good addiction. I

simply have to get out there every day; it's just who I am. I'm also a social runner, I'll run with anyone. I often get a kick out of some of the young 'hot shots' who call me to ask if they can run with our small group. I tell them that we meet every day at 4:00 o'clock at the corner of Mahantongo and Twentieth Street in Pottsville, and that they're more than welcome to join us. They usually show up and last about a week. Knowing that I've run in most of the major marathons, many of the young runners will ask me how much I trained when I was competing at that level. They think I'm kidding when I tell them that I would run eighty to a hundred miles a week, and some weeks even up to a hundred and twenty."

Aside from the simple love of the sport, Joe also talked about the friendships he made throughout his career. He talks about traveling to Chambersburg, PA every year to run in the race of a friend whose father started a running club many years ago and who passed away at the age of sixty-five. His son has a memorial race yearly that attracts between 700 and 800 runners. "I look forward, every year, to go down there to meet old friends and to run in the race. The camaraderie associated with the sport is another reason why I could never give it up."

Joe believes running is a great sport for anyone at any age, simply because everyone can do it. Whether you're training for a marathon or getting in that mile or two each morning to start off your day, it's worth every step.

I often hear guys in their twenties reliving their glory days of high school. It's sad to think that life has stopped for these individuals the day they received their diplomas. I feel sorry for those who have quit long before they should, and I'm not just talking about the field of sports; I'm talking about life, and the will to go on. People today need to focus on and teach the next generation to focus on things that they can control and not worry about the things they can't. Getting older is not a bad thing, and it affects all of us whether we want to accept it or not. We need to appreciate the past, but more importantly we need to embrace the future. Memories are not the key to getting old, but making new memories, regardless of age, is a reason to live and to live well. Each day is a new frontier with new challenges and new experiences. Wake up every morning and be ready to take on a new adventure, meet a new person, laugh at something funny or cry at something sad.

Life is a lot like athletics. Regardless of the sport, the single most important driving force that keeps many athletes going long past their prime is the feeling of knowing they can still push themselves. The soreness is the medal they will receive after every workout, and the feeling of accomplishment is the treasure. It doesn't matter how they get it done. What matters is they get it done, and they savor the feeling. It's the attitude, the carrot that is just outside their reach. It's accepting the challenge of colleagues who keep reminding them they're too old to be doing the things they're doing, the things that keep the juices flowing and the attitude alive.

I had the great pleasure of reaching the half century mark in January 2003. The day of the week was a Monday, and our school day was a teacher development day, meaning the students had the day off. The teachers on the other hand had a full day working on curriculum and attending various meetings with our respective departments and administrators. We had an hour for lunch, so I made it a point to recruit some of our faculty members to celebrate my birthday by playing a little three-on-three basketball during our lunch break. We also talked a few of the high school players into showing up for the eleven o'clock workout, just to be sure that we had enough guys.

After some friendly jeering about the old man, we began playing. It didn't take long until we got down to business. We played about four or five games of eleven points and by the second game we all forgot about ages and receding hairlines and concentrated on playing the game all out. I didn't realize until I lay in bed that night, a little sore and pretty tired, that I wouldn't have wanted to turn fifty any other way. We always have that same itinerary the last day of school. The students finish their final exams by eleven a.m. and at high noon our "End of the Year" pickup games begin. This past year our old regulars showed up and, once again, we invited some of the high school players from our school. I also asked my nephew, who plays for a rival high school in the same league, to show up and to bring a friend or two. We had an outstanding hour and a half battle of four-on-four. When it was over and I was bent over, totally exhausted, it was great to look over and see the young guys crouching in the same position. Before anyone departed that afternoon, I called them all together and thanked them all for showing up, and I reminded them just how great the game is. I told the young players to take a look around. There are no fans in the bleachers; no coaches barking out orders, no referees, cheerleaders, or parents, just a bunch of guys from different schools and different generations getting together to go at it.

I asked them how much they enjoyed the workout and every one of them said, to borrow a modern phrase— *AWESOME.* I told them this is the kind of thing, and it saddens me to say it, their generation is missing. The idea of getting a group of guys together, regardless of your school affiliation, to play some serious half court basketball is well worth a couple of phone calls. I told them, "I'm not talking about grabbing a bunch of guys who aren't players. I'm talking about guys who take the game seriously and who want to get better. I'm talking about guys who will come running when they hear there's a game to be played. I'm talking about you guys."

I must confess that for me and my fellow faculty members, it's without a doubt the best way to end the school year. The day for us doesn't end with a hot shower, however. After this traditional workout, we proceed to the home of one of our faculty players and break out the lawn chairs and a few cold ones to celebrate the end of another school year. It doesn't take long for the conversation to drift to the young kids who came back to play that day, and we always speak of them with a sense of admiration. As the afternoon blissfully lingers on and that "good soreness" starts to creep in, there's a smile on each of our faces as we promise each other, if our arms and legs are still moving 365 days from now, we'll be at it again.

To all you jocks out there who are closing in on the half century mark, and to those of you who have already passed it, I'm making a personal challenge to you to put the remote down and get out of the recliner. Take a walk or a slow run, play some golf, catch a little baseball with your kids, or swim a few laps in the pool. I promise you the feeling you'll have when you finish will make it all worth while.

Those who have never been there cannot appreciate it. Those who have tasted it time and time again, that good soreness, that feeling of physical accomplishment, can only understand its magic.

# THE FUTURE

The greatest compliment that can be given to a young basketball player is to be labeled a "gym rat". A gym rat can best be defined as a player who lives for the game. They're often recognized by the tape covering the toes of their sneakers. They wear worn out gym shorts and old tee shirts, and they can be found from morning till night in their respected playgrounds and school yards.

Many have a record of misdemeanors for finding ways into local gyms long after the doors are locked and the lights are turned off. Though some big men may have the needed credentials, the label is usually attached to guards. It must have to do with the terminology depicting the rat as a small, nasty animal that should not be cornered. Gym rats take charges; they dive for loose balls, and their knees and elbows are always covered with scabs. Players outside of the fraternity usually do not want to play against them. Teammates put their trust in them, and coaches swear by them, trying to get less enthusiastic players to follow their example.

Jim Valvano's camp speeches always made reference to

them. He would make comparisons between the gym rats and the big timers. He would tell the campers he was the ultimate gym rat. He loved to coach these types of players because they were just like him.

Gym rats cannot be created; they simply exist. My concern, or should I say fear, is that this well defined athlete may one day face extinction. The gym rat must be preserved if the game is going to survive and flourish. We cannot force kids today to fall in love with the game. What we can and must do is re-emphasize the "fun of the game", a phrase that seems to have lost it's meaning in the realm of basketball today.

We need to allow kids the opportunity to play the game without outside interference. Kids need to get their juices flowing with a healthy dose of competition, created and fostered by none other than themselves. They need to feel the exhilaration associated with making that great pass or finishing a fast break, that was not designed from a playbook or a coach. They need to know the respect that goes along with playing hard, the exhilaration of playing to win as a team member, and the understanding that the team doesn't have to consist of five players. They need to develop friendships and build reputations that can be foundations for their futures. They need to play pickup games, and pickup games, and more pickup games. Young players today need space, and they need reassurance that the game isn't life-altering or future-driven.

WHEN THE GAME WAS JUST A GAME

We old timers need to take it upon ourselves to invite some of the high school and junior high players into our twice a week pickup games. We need to tell them stories, even exaggerated ones, of the grand old days of the game. We need to pass on traditions associated with the game, and we need to make it known to them that they have an obligation to keep those traditions alive. We cannot allow the game itself to be lost to the "bottom line" mentality that has become a cancer eating away at the games' very core.

Is there still hope for the future of our game? I believe there is. I believe it when I see a gym rat's knees and elbows covered with brush burns from diving for loose balls. I believe it every time I see a pair of worn out sneakers on a kid who, regardless of criticisms and outside interferences, still plays the game with an unbridled passion. I believe it every time I hear Thursday night pick-up games that are still being played, and I hope and pray that some of the new generation will continue the tradition. I believe it every time I hear Dick Vitale, the passionate color commentator for ESPN college basketball, talk about having the greatest job in the world. Yes, I believe there's hope. If I didn't, I never would have taken on the challenge of writing this book. Many of the basketball people I interviewed have restored my faith. I've learned there is a general concern out there for the game and there is also a fear among the true believers that the game could be slipping away. We need to take it upon ourselves to promote the game, with a hope and conviction to make the positives far outweigh the negatives.

Will the game itself return to the way it was a generation ago? I don't believe it will. I don't believe professional basketball will ever raise the age limit for entering the NBA draft. I don't believe we will ever see NBA teams being comprised of the same nucleus of players as in past generations.

Salaries are out of control, and the financial golden ring is, and probably always will be, the primary motivation to the young players of today. I read an article once about Paul Arizon, the Hall of Famer who grew up in Philadelphia, graduated from Villanova University, and went on to an illustrious career with the Philadelphia Warriors. The article mentioned Arizon's top salary between 1952 and 1960 as being somewhere in the vicinity of $30,000, prompting him to take a job in the off season. Could you imagine today's NBA players working a second job to subsidize their incomes? Ariizon talked about playing the game back then for the love of the game, not for the money. He actually was offered more money to relocate but he was a Philly guy who took pride in playing for his home city.

Still, my faith is strongly reinforced, when I read about those driven players in the semi-pro leagues dreaming of their shot, of the many players who head for foreign soil, battling the language barriers and missing home cooking in the hopes of hooking up with a foreign team, rather than giving up on their dream. There's still a few of the NBA veterans like Jason Kidd and Grant Hill, who continue to compete like youngsters because its still a game to them, and we need to take a note from them. Yes, I believe the professional game can survive, but a wake-up call is definitely in order.

The excitement of the NCAA tournament will not allow the college game to die. Regardless of the underclass-dominated programs, and the realization that teams that are not made up of the best college age players in the land, the excitement will remain. March Madness is still the pinnacle of college sports. Maybe it's the fact the 64 teams, or should I say 65, that comprise the NCAA tournament, provide more people in more areas of the country with a reason to cheer for their favorite teams.

I mentioned that I am from Northeastern Pennsylvania. I'm amazed but not surprised how the city of Scranton was enthralled by the journey of Syracuse basketball and native son Gerry McNamara's freshman season. It was March 2003, and Syracuse was heading to New Orleans to do battle with Texas, while Marquette would take on Kansas, in the Final Four. Although most of the nation was looking at Marquette as the sentimental favorite, the fans from Scranton would say, "Don't even go there." The following of Gerry Mac was simply fantastic; as I'm sure it was in the hometowns of other college stars who were heading to the Big Easy. Could it be that fans find it easier to align themselves with teams made up of nonprofessionals, with schools and conferences that have molded rivalries over decades of memorable moments and overtime classics? Or does the college game give people a reason to follow a native born high school legend into the Final Four?

My concern is not with the professional or the college game. My fear is for the future of the game, the next level down, and even more so with the levels below that. High school, junior high, grade school, biddy leagues and all the places that young boys and girls are participating have to be the targeted areas. The survival or devastation of our game will depend on how the future will treat our younger athletes. We somehow need to come to grips with the fact that young people need exercise, and keeping them involved in athletics should supercede their talent or lack of. We cannot allow kids to be ranked as the top 3$^{rd}$ or 4$^{th}$ grade kid in our country. In fact, we cannot allow kids to be ranked as the top 3$^{rd}$ or 4$^{th}$ grade kid on their biddy league team. The more that young people are rejected at these lower levels, the less you'll hear the ball bouncing in those grade school gyms and neighborhood playgrounds. I urge adults to take a ride by these playgrounds and see the broken concrete and the weeds protruding through the cracks, and know that the problem with their lack of use may start with you. We need to give the kids of today hope. We owe it to them.

# EPILOGUE

As athletes, we place a certain value and importance on the sport or sports we've come to love. We follow our favorite teams, read about the star performers, and most of all still participate, at one level or another, often dealing with Father Time as our greatest challenge. As time moves on, most of us come to the realization that the game, any game, has to be programmed into a time slot. The early morning run, the aerobics class, the time set aside for the treadmill, or the weekly pickup game, too often is squeezed into our busy schedules. To us older athletes, the game or the workout is something we cherish.

The competition, the physical challenge, the friendships and camaraderie shared by a group of athletes is of great value to us all. We need to instill this virtue into today's athletes, and we need to stress upon them, and maybe even ourselves, that athletics needs to be put into proper perspective. Athletes need to realize the world is not over if they're cut from a team, or if an injury sidelines them or even cuts short their careers. A sport is just that, a sport, but life and life's decisions travel with us far from the playing fields and gymnasiums, and we need to come to the realization there are more pressing issues facing us today.

A few years ago, while working a basketball camp in Southern Virginia, I was given a lesson in "sport's reality". A friend of mine who was one of the directors of the camp told me a story about some recent events that he claims were the most stressful of his life. He is the athletic director of a large High School in Northern Virginia and it was the preceding fall when the city of Washington and the surrounding areas were being terrorized by two men committing sniper attacks. He said many of the areas being viewed nationally on T.V. were in and around his school district. As the police wondered where the snipers would attack next, he talked about the helpless feeling and fear he felt each time he stopped for gas or had to make a decision whether or not to allow his own children to go outside to play. Being an athletic director did not lesson the pressure. Having to schedule outdoor sporting events for the many fall programs was mind boggling. He said he and many of the other A.D.'s in the surrounding area even began changing the times and sites of games, hoping that the confusion and misdirection might thwart off any planned attacks and create a somewhat safer atmosphere. He claimed they even went so far as to move games to different parts of the state and to play them at different times than originally scheduled.

As the sports' seasons progressed, and the sniper

attacks continued, the growing tension was becoming unbearable. For him and his school, the reality peaked on a Saturday afternoon in Southern Virginia. My friend and the A.D. from an opposing Northern Virginia school district mutually decided to move a football game to a site in the southern part of the state. The game was scheduled to be played on a Saturday morning at 11:00 a.m., and the location was kept from the public as long as possible. The game was played in front of a scarce crowd, made up primarily of parents who ventured south that morning, and the game proceeded without a hitch. My friend admitted that he was relieved, as he was with all the outside events taking place that fall, when the teams were off the field. He said when all was completed, he and his family got into his car and headed home. Later that afternoon, he received a phone call from the football coach who seemed very upset. The coach asked him if he was watching the news and did he see the breaking developments. A shooting took place in the parking lot of a Ponderosa Steak House restaurant in Ashland, Virginia, just off Route 95. The coach informed him that the team decided to stop and eat at that very restaurant and had departed the parking lot just a short time before the incident occurred. My friend, the A.D, said he couldn't stop thinking of what could have happened with a whole team full of high school kids in that parking lot, if they would have played the game an hour or so later that Saturday. As a nation, we were all relieved when the snipers were finally apprehended, but to my friend from Northern Virginia, the reality of sport took on an entirely different meaning.

Putting the game of basketball and all sport into proper perspective may be the key to their survival. I started writing this chapter on April 5, 2003. The previous night I had the pleasure of coaching a team made up of eighth grade boys, including my own son, in a tournament run by an organization called Athletes for Better Education. Our number system for substitutions worked well. The game was an exciting one, and we lost by four points. The kids were down for a minute or two, but knowing the tournament was a double elimination format and they would have a chance to play again tomorrow seemed to rekindle their spirits and charge up their batteries. Parents seemed happy and were supportive, as they should be. All in all it was an enjoyable evening.

The reason I brought up the date of this game has to do with the relative levity of its importance. Earlier that same day the U.S. Armed Forces took over the Saddam Hussien Airport and changed it to the Baghdad Airport. Coalition forces of Operation Enduring Freedom had just entered the city of Baghdad with the hope of ending the war. Returning from our game that evening I turned on the national news for an update, and watching the pictures of American soldiers fighting their way across the desert of Iraq hit me square between the eyes with a shot of reality. This particular Saturday was also the day of the Final

Four, college basketball's ultimate showcase, yet the games didn't quite hold the magic in lieu of the circumstances surrounding our world.

It's important every now and then to take a step back and examine the events that truly determine our lives and to try to arrange those events into their proper places. We, sometimes, need to minimize the importance of a mere sporting event as compared to the game of life, yet so many of us cannot. I urge everyone, if not for themselves then for the kids of this generation and for the ones to follow, to take a reality check. Putting things into their proper perspective is not easy in this day and age, but it is crucial. We find it difficult to put a chronological order to our own lives, when so much around us is out of order. I once heard Charles Barkley comment on being a hero. He said that teachers, doctors, people who have an impact on the way others live are the ones who are heroes. Sir Charles referred to himself a basketball player who got paid very well for playing a game that he happened to be good at.

It's often hard for us to comprehend the fact that many professional athletes are paid more than the President of the United States. I'm not begrudging anyone for capitalizing on their talents, but where has it left us in comparison to our own importance? How many parents would rather see their children become professional athletes instead of teachers, doctors, or even the President of the United States? Where does our youth draw the line when it comes to perspective in their lives? Could it have something to do with the reason so many young people today are quitting sports at a young age? Could it be why dropout rates in our schools continue to climb? Could it be why more and more young people are giving up at a time when they should be waking up and facing a world full of remarkable changes and opportunities?

Yes, I think the game of basketball, as well as other sports, was better a generation ago. I truly believe there was less pressure surrounding it, and there was much less outside interference. I also believe that our lives were a little simpler back then, for we were able to put things into perspective better than we are today.

At the time I wrote this paragraph, I didn't know if my eighth grade team would still be alive in their double elimination tournament game scheduled for that afternoon. I did know that for my part, as the coach of the team, all the kids would play and have some fun. I also knew when the game was over, I would go home and watch the Final Four and root for Syracuse and Gerry McNamara of Scranton, Pa. to win. But more important, I knew that, before I would go to bed that night, I would end my day tuning into the war in Iraq, the real game, the one that would put everything else into proper perspective. I also knew I would get down on my knees and thank God that I'm an American, and I would pray for my team over in Iraq to "WIN IT ALL"!

# REFERENCES

Valvano—Jim Valvano and Curry Kirkparick—Pocket Books 1991

Sports Illustrated—2/13/95—Mccullum, Jack—Gelin, Dave—Out of Joint

Sports Illustrated—4/12/99—Rick Reilly—Funny You Should Ask

And The Crowd Goes Wild—Library of Congress Cataloging—Publication Data—Garner, Joe 1999

The Last Amateurs—John Feinstein—Little, Brown and Co. 2000

Just Let the Kids Play—Bob Bigelow, Tom Moroney, and Linda Hall—Health Communications Inc. 2001

Sports Illustrated—11/25/02—Rick Reilly—Dribblephelia

Philadelphia Daily News—2/6/02 The Collegians—Jerardi, Jack

Washington Post—2'24'03—A New Meaning of Playground Basketball—Williams, Preston

Sports Illustrated—9/22/03 Rick Reilly—The Fat of the Land

Printed in the United States
143653LV00011B/2/P